P9-DGM-166

CORE VALUES

SETTING MY MORAL COMPASS

	ENTRY LEVEL	ADVANCED LEVEL
SESSION 1 Orientation	Be-Attitudes Matthew 5:1–12	
SESSION 2 Morality	A Moral Dilemma? Matthew 5:21–37	Children of God Romans 8:5–17
SESSION 3 Unconditional Love	Revenge and Love Matthew 5:38–48	Building Community Phil. 1:12–18a,27–2:4
SESSION 4 Spirituality	Give, Pray, Fast Matthew 6:1–18	Living by the Spirit Galatians 5:16–26
SESSION 5 Contentment	Not to Worry Matthew 6:19–34	Planning Ahead 1 Timothy 6:3–19
SESSION 6 Relationships	Judge or Judged? Matthew 7:1–12	Life Together James 4:1–12
SESSION 7 Choices	Building Plans Matthew 7:13–27	A Piece of the Rock 1 Cor. 3:1–23

Serendipity House / P.O. Box 1012 / Littleton, CO 80160

TOLL FREE 1-800-525-9563 / www.serendipityhouse.com

© 1992, 1998 Serendipity House. All rights reserved.

98 99 00 01 / **101 series** • **CHG** / 4 3 2

PROJECT ENGINEER:
Lyman Coleman

WRITING TEAM:
Richard Peace, Lyman Coleman, Andrew Sloan, Cathy Tardif

PRODUCTION TEAM:
Christopher Werner, Sharon Penington, Erika Tiepel

COVER PHOTO:
© Barry Rosenthal / FPG International, LLC.

CORE VALUES

Community:	The purpose of this curriculum is to build community within the body of believers around Jesus Christ.
Group Process:	To build community, the curriculum must be designed to take a group through a step-by-step process of sharing your story with one another.
Interactive Bible Study:	To share your "story," the approach to Scripture in the curriculum needs to be open-ended and right brain—to "level the playing field" and encourage everyone to share.
Developmental Stages:	To provide a healthy program in the life cycle of a group, the curriculum needs to offer courses on three levels of commitment: (1) Beginner Stage—low-level entry, high structure, to level the playing field; (2) Growth Stage—deeper Bible study, flexible structure, to encourage group accountability; (3) Discipleship Stage—in-depth Bible study, open structure, to move the group into high gear.
Target Audiences:	To build community throughout the culture of the church, the curriculum needs to be flexible, adaptable and transferable into the structure of the average church.

ACKNOWLEDGMENTS

To Zondervan Bible Publishers
for permission to use
the NIV text,
The Holy Bible, New International Bible Society.
© 1973, 1978, 1984 by International Bible Society.
Used by permission of Zondervan Bible Publishers.

Questions and Answers

PURPOSE

1. What is the purpose of this group?

In a nutshell, the purpose is to get acquainted and to double the size of the group.

STAGE

2. What stage in the life cycle of a small group is this course designed for?

This 101 course is designed for the first stage in the three-stage life cycle of a small group. (See diagram below.) For a full explanation of the three-stage life cycle, see the center section.

GOALS

3. What is the purpose of stage one in the life cycle?

The focus in this first stage is primarily on Group Building.

GROUP BUILDING

4. How does this course develop Group Building?

Take a look at the illustration of the baseball diamond on page M5 in the center section. In the process of using this course, you will go around the four bases.

BIBLE STUDY

5. What is the approach to Bible Study in this course?

As shown on page M4 of the center section, there are two tracks in this book. Track 1 is the light option, based on stories in the Bible. Track 2 is the heavier option, based on teaching passages in the Bible.

THREE-STAGE LIFE CYCLE OF A GROUP

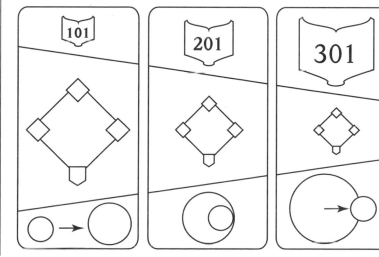

3

6. **Which option of Bible Study is best for our group?**

Track 1 is the best option for people not familiar with the Bible, as well as for groups who are not familiar with each other. Track 2 is the best option for groups who are familiar with the Bible *and* with one another. (However, whenever you have new people come to a meeting, we recommend you switch to Track 1 for that Bible Study.)

7. **Can we choose both options?**

Yes, depending upon your time schedule. Here's how to decide:

STUDY	APPROXIMATE COMPLETION TIME
Story Sharing only	60–90 minutes
Epistle Study only	60–90 minutes
Story and Epistle Study	90–120 minutes

8. **What if we want to do both the Story and Epistle Studies but don't have time at the session?**

You can spend two weeks on a unit—the Story Questionnaire the first week and the Epistle Study the next. Session 1 has only one Bible Study—so you would end up with 13 weeks if you followed this plan.

9. **What if you don't know anything about the Bible?**

No problem. The Story option is based on a parable or story that stands on its own—to discuss as though you are hearing it for the first time. The Epistle Study comes with complete reference notes—to help you understand the context of the Bible passage and any difficult words that need to be defined.

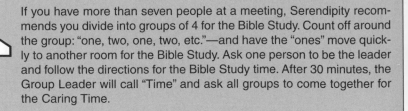

THE FEARLESS FOURSOME!

If you have more than seven people at a meeting, Serendipity recommends you divide into groups of 4 for the Bible Study. Count off around the group: "one, two, one, two, etc."—and have the "ones" move quickly to another room for the Bible Study. Ask one person to be the leader and follow the directions for the Bible Study time. After 30 minutes, the Group Leader will call "Time" and ask all groups to come together for the Caring Time.

**MISSION /
MULTIPLICATION**

O→O

10. What is the mission of a 101 group?

Turn to page M5 of the center section. This course is designed for groups in the Birth stage—which means that your mission is to increase the size of the group by filling the "empty chair."

**THE EMPTY
CHAIR**

11. How do we fill the empty chair?

Pull up an empty chair during the group's prayer time and ask God to bring a new person to the group to fill it.

**GROUP
COVENANT**

12. What is a group covenant?

A group covenant is a "contract" that spells out your expectations and the ground rules for your group. It's very important that your group discuss these issues—preferably as part of the first session.

**GROUND
RULES**

13. What are the ground rules for the group? (Check those that you agree upon.)

❐ PRIORITY: While you are in the course, you give the group meetings priority.

❐ PARTICIPATION: Everyone participates and no one dominates.

❐ RESPECT: Everyone is given the right to their own opinion and all questions are encouraged and respected.

❐ CONFIDENTIALITY: Anything that is said in the meeting is never repeated outside the meeting.

❐ EMPTY CHAIR: The group stays open to new people at every meeting.

❐ SUPPORT: Permission is given to call upon each other in time of need—even in the middle of the night.

❐ ADVICE GIVING: Unsolicited advice is not allowed.

❐ MISSION: We agree to do everything in our power to start a new group as our mission (see center section).

SESSION
1

Orientation

3-PART AGENDA

ICE-BREAKER
15 Minutes

BIBLE STUDY
30 Minutes

CARING TIME
15–45 Minutes

Today many "experts" offer "road maps" to happiness. True happiness and contentment can be elusive. We may be happy when we are with family or friends, shopping, achieving a goal, receiving an award or getting our own way. But afterward we return to discontentment and unhappiness. The reason—we seek happiness, not joy. Happiness is temporal; joy is eternal. Happiness is based on earthly circumstances; joy is based on spiritual realities. Happiness is dependent on external events; joy is an inner reality.

In order to achieve joy, we need to change our paradigm. A paradigm is the lens through which we see the world. The word "paradigm" is a Greek word, and means the way in which we perceive, understand and interpret the world around us. Real change occurs from the inside out. The Sermon on the Mount is a new lens Christ gives us through which we see our world. It

> **LEADER: Be sure to read the "Questions and Answers" on pages 3–5. Take some time during this first session to have the group go over the ground rules on page 5. At the beginning of the Caring Time have your group look at pages M1–M3 in the center section of this book.**

is not a new way **of** seeing the world; it is a new way **to** see the world. This course is about discovering the core values—the moral compass—which will help us to change from the inside out. We must start with ourselves—how we view the world (paradigm), and how we function and respond in the world (our character and our motives).

In our studies, we will look at some of the ways Scripture challenges our perspective and our thinking. The Option 1 studies focus on the Sermon on the Mount and our Lord's teachings about developing a Christlike character. The Option 2 studies look at the writings of Paul and James. Their writings instruct us on the way they developed their inner character in the midst of their culture.

In this course, the Bible Study approach is a little unique with a different focus. Usually, the content of the passage is the focus of the Bible Study. In this course, the focus will be on telling your "story," using the passage as a springboard.

Every session has three parts: (1) **Ice-Breaker**—to break the ice and introduce the topic, (2) **Bible Study**—to share your own life through a passage of Scripture, and (3) **Caring Time**—to share prayer concerns and pray for one another.

Ice-Breaker / 15 Minutes

A Day in the Life ... There would probably be no better way to get to know a person than to follow them around for a day. Since we cannot do that very easily with each other, we'll do the next best thing—share what a typical day in our life is like. Do so by completing the following sentences:

1. Generally it's best to not talk to me in the morning before ...
- ❏ I've had my cup of coffee.
- ❏ noon!
- ❏ No problem—I'm a morning person.
- ❏ I've read my paper.
- ❏ I've had my shower.
- ❏ other:_____

2. The high point of my day is when ...
- ❏ my kids go to school.
- ❏ my kids come home.
- ❏ my spouse comes home.
- ❏ I get to delve into my pet project.
- ❏ I come home.
- ❏ I talk to my friend(s).
- ❏ I get to eat.
- ❏ other:_____

3. An important part of ending my day is ...
- ❏ watching a favorite TV show.
- ❏ watching the news.
- ❏ prayer and quiet time.
- ❏ reflecting on the day with my spouse.
- ❏ watching the sunset.
- ❏ reading.
- ❏ other:_____

Bible Study / 30 Minutes

Matthew 5:1–12 / Be-Attitudes

Read the following Scripture from Jesus' opening words in the Sermon on the Mount. The Sermon on the Mount is a collection of sayings which focus on the character and actions that mark those who are disciples of Jesus. The Sermon begins with what are known as the Beatitudes. The

Beatitudes describe what kind of person God wants us to be, and then declares the rewards such a person can expect. Discuss your responses to the questions with your group. Be sure to save time at the close to discuss the issues in the Caring Time.

5 Now when he saw the crowds, he went up on a mountainside and sat down. His disciples came to him, ²and he began to teach them, saying:
³"Blessed are the poor in spirit,
    for theirs is the kingdom of heaven.
⁴Blessed are those who mourn,
    for they will be comforted.
⁵Blessed are the meek,
    for they will inherit the earth.
⁶Blessed are those who hunger and thirst for righteousness,
    for they will be filled.
⁷Blessed are the merciful,
    for they will be shown mercy.
⁸Blessed are the pure in heart,
    for they will see God.
⁹Blessed are the peacemakers,
    for they will be called sons of God.
¹⁰Blessed are those who are persecuted because of righteousness,
    for theirs is the kingdom of heaven.

¹¹"Blessed are you when people insult you, persecute you and falsely say all kinds of evil against you because of me. ¹²Rejoice and be glad, because great is your reward in heaven, for in the same way they persecuted the prophets who were before you."

1. Imagine that you were sitting on the hillside that day with the disciples. What would be your first impression after hearing Jesus' words?
❒ What on earth is he talking about?
❒ This guy doesn't live in the real world.
❒ Jesus had better change his message—because he won't get very far preaching that stuff.
❒ This lifestyle is what I have been searching for.

2. When you were 7 years old, which of these "children's beatitudes" would have applied to you?
❒ "Blessed are those who bake me cookies and treats."
❒ "Blessed are those who don't put me down."
❒ "Blessed are those who move next door with children my age."
❒ "Blessed are those who listen to what I have to say."
❒ "Blessed are those adults who make time to play with me."
❒ "Blessed are those who teach me right from wrong."
❒ "Blessed are those who show me who Jesus is."

3. Who fulfilled one of these "children's beatitudes" for you?

4. My reaction to being "poor in spirit," "mourning," being "meek" and being "persecuted" is:
   ❐ I'm feeling kind of depressed—do we really have to do this?
   ❐ I'm intrigued to find out what Jesus is attempting to do.
   ❐ These terms need to be defined further for me.
   ❐ I've lived with these values long enough to know that this lifestyle is really "blessed."
   ❐ I'm confused—this sounds unbalanced and not very attractive.
   ❐ other:_____

5. Are the Beatitudes applicable to life today, or really only to the lives of Jesus' audience? How do these promised blessings compare with what most people in the world prize?

6. Silently take the following "attitude check" by placing the appropriate number (from 1 to 4) in the space next to each beatitude.

1	2	3	4
I'm just beginning.	I'm making progress.	I've experienced this.	This is part of my life.

___POOR IN SPIRIT: I recognize my spiritual bankruptcy and my need for God. Because my relationship with God depends on his grace, I know I'm incapable of earning God's love on my own.

___MOURN: I feel the pain that sin, including my own, causes. I can let others know when I am hurting without embarrassment. I can weep like Jesus did.

___MEEK: I don't have to be the strong one who is always in control. I can be tender and gentle. I've given control of my life to God and I don't always have to win.

___SPIRITUAL HUNGER: I want to know God and his will for my life more than anything—including my own pleasure, status or success. My heart truly longs for God.

___MERCIFUL: I can share the feelings of people who are hurting, lonely or distressed, and walk alongside them in their pain. God has given me a sensitivity for the suffering of others and a compassion to help them.

___PURE IN HEART: I am completely honest with God and others. I don't have to put on a false front or pretend to be something I'm not. My life is marked with openness and integrity.

"God cannot give us happiness and peace apart from himself, because it is not there. There is no such thing."
—C.S. Lewis

____PEACEMAKER: I work hard to keep channels of communication open with others. Rather than allowing anger and conflict to fester, I deal with them constructively. I help those around me work out their differences without hurting one another.

____PERSECUTION: I know for whom and for what I am living. And for this I am willing to suffer and (if need be) stand alone for what is right. I can take criticism without reacting defensively or feeling self-pity.

7. Share with the group which beatitude you would rate as your highest and which beatitude you would rate as your lowest.

8. What do you need to change in order for your life to reflect the Beatitudes?
   ❏ I need to change the way I view the world.
   ❏ I need to change my attitude.
   ❏ I need to change my behavior.
   ❏ I need to change my circumstances.
   ❏ I need to continue what I am doing, since my life already reflects the Beatitudes.
   ❏ other:_____

COMMENT

The Sermon on the Mount (Matt. 5:1–7:29), like the Ten Commandments, is one of the best-known passages in the Bible. Many people are at least somewhat familiar with the Beatitudes, the Lord's Prayer, the admonition to "consider the lilies of the field," and the parable about the two men who built their houses on sand and on rock.

The Sermon on the Mount has been described as "the best definition of the mental attitude of someone who has turned over his or her life to God." The word "blessed" is often translated as "happy" or "healthy." The attitudes described by Jesus may sound old-fashioned and even contradictory, but modern psychiatry is reconsidering its definition of happiness. Some of its assertions echo what Jesus has to say here.

The Beatitudes are not defining eight different types of people but the characteristics that are to be found in every child of God. While there is a tension in this section (and throughout the Sermon) between the ideal (presented here) and the real (the presence of sin and failure), Jesus is here defining the character that is to be formed in his disciples.

Caring Time / 15–45 Minutes

The most important time in every meeting is this—the CARING TIME—where you take time to share prayer requests and pray for one another. To make sure this time is not neglected, you need to set a minimum time that you will devote to prayer requests and prayer and count backward from the closing time by this amount. For instance, if you are going to close at 9 p.m., and you are going to devote 30 minutes to prayer requests and prayer, you need to ask a timekeeper to call "time" at 8:30 and move to prayer requests. Start out by asking everyone to answer this question:

"How can we help you in prayer this week?"

Then, move into prayer. If you have not prayed out loud before, finish this sentence:

"Hello, God, this is ... (first name). I want to thank you for ..."

Be sure to pray for the empty chair. And as you do, think about who you could invite to join you as you begin this study.

LEADER: Ask the group, "Who are you going to invite next week?"

GROUP DIRECTORY

P.S.
At the close, pass around your books and have everyone sign the GROUP DIRECTORY inside the front cover.

SESSION
2

Morality

3-PART AGENDA

ICE-BREAKER
15 Minutes

BIBLE STUDY
30 Minutes

CARING TIME
15–45 Minutes

When we deal with issues of morality, we know there will be great discussions or heated arguments. Give 10 people a case study on anger, adultery or divorce, and you will hear 10 different opinions on the case. And they all may be based on different rationales. How do we decide what is moral within such a confusing context?

There is a tension between the way things are (realities), and the way things should be (values). As people of faith, our responsibility is to emphasize the way things should be—the values which faith teaches us. This means we see moral issues through the glasses of our values, rather than the spectacles of society. Granted, our perception may be influenced by our culture—it's so pervasive that sometimes it is hard to see how much it influences our thinking. The key is to focus on God, whose teaching and righteousness transcends all culture. If we allow God to change us from the inside out, we develop a Christlike character and we will have a deep moral base. Then our attitudes and actions will reflect our changed inner character.

LEADER: *If there are new people in this session, review the ground rules for this group on page 5. Have the group look at page M4 in the center section and decide which Bible Study option to use— light or heavy. If you have more than seven people, see the box about the "Fearless Foursome" on page 4.*

In the Option 1 Study (from the Sermon on the Mount in Matthew), Jesus tackles head-on the tough moral issues of anger, adultery and divorce. In the Option 2 Study, Paul (in his letter to the Romans) describes the life of one who lives by the Spirit and not under the Old Testament Law.

To get started, take a few minutes and answer the questions in the following ice-breaker. Be sure to save plenty of time at the end of this session for the CARING TIME—to share your concerns and pray for one another. This is what this course is all about.

Ice-Breaker / 15 Minutes

Life Signs. Spend some time thinking about your lives in terms of traffic signs. Have each person share their response to each question.

1. If you were to select a traffic sign to tell how you've been seeking to live your life, what sign would it be?
   - ❐ "Merge"—because I've been trying to get along with everyone
   - ❐ "Slow"—because I've been seeking to slow down and experience more of life
   - ❐ "Keep Right"—because I'm trying to keep my life on the right track
   - ❐ "No U-Turn"—because I'm resisting the urge to go back to the past
   - ❐ "One Way"—because I'm seeking to be more decisive in my life
   - ❐ "Yield"—because I'm seeking to yield my life to God
   - ❐ "Children Playing"—because I'm trying to let out the "child" in me
   - ❐ "Under Construction"—because I'm changing so much

2. What sign are you displaying in your relationship with others?
   - ❐ "No Trespassing!"—because I keep people at a distance
   - ❐ "Help Wanted"—because I'm reaching out for support
   - ❐ "One Way"—because I'm not always tolerant of differences
   - ❐ "Open 24 Hours"—because I'm always available to others
   - ❐ "Keep Right"—because I encourage others to do what is right
   - ❐ "No Vacancy"—because there's no room in my life for anyone else right now

3. If God were to give you a "traffic ticket" right now for how you are living your life, what would it be for?
   - ❐ "Speeding"—not slowing down enough to really live
   - ❐ "Failing to Yield"—trying to do things my own way
   - ❐ "Blocking Traffic"—I feel I've gotten in the way of others who are doing more.
   - ❐ "Illegal U-Turn"—I have been trying to live in the past.
   - ❐ "Driving the Wrong Way on a One-Way Street"—I need to turn my life around.

Bible Study / 30 Minutes

Option 1 / Gospel Study

Matthew 5:21–37 / A Moral Dilemma?

Jesus shows that righteousness is not a matter of conforming to regulations, but comes from focusing on what is going on in one's heart. Read Matthew 5:21–37 and discuss your responses to the questions with your group.

[21] *"You have heard that it was said to the people long ago, 'Do not murder, and anyone who murders will be subject to judgment.'* [22] *But I tell you that anyone who is angry with his brother will be subject to judgment. Again, anyone who says to his brother, 'Raca,' is answerable to the Sanhedrin. But anyone who says, 'You fool!' will be in danger of the fire of hell.*

[23] *"Therefore, if you are offering your gift at the altar and there remember that your brother has something against you,* [24] *leave your gift there in front of the altar. First go and be reconciled to your brother; then come and offer your gift.*

[25] *"Settle matters quickly with your adversary who is taking you to court. Do it while you are still with him on the way, or he may hand you over to the judge, and the judge may hand you over to the officer, and you may be thrown into prison.* [26] *I tell you the truth, you will not get out until you have paid the last penny.*

[27] *"You have heard that it was said, 'Do not commit adultery.'* [28] *But I tell you that anyone who looks at a woman lustfully has already committed adultery with her in his heart.* [29] *If your right eye causes you to sin, gouge it out and throw it away. It is better for you to lose one part of your body than for your whole body to be thrown into hell.* [30] *And if your right hand causes you to sin, cut it off and throw it away. It is better for you to lose one part of your body than for your whole body to go into hell.*

[31] *"It has been said, 'Anyone who divorces his wife must give her a certificate of divorce.'* [32] *But I tell you that anyone who divorces his wife, except for marital unfaithfulness, causes her to become an adulteress, and anyone who marries the divorced woman commits adultery.*

[33] *"Again, you have heard that it was said to the people long ago, 'Do not break your oath, but keep the oaths you have made to the Lord.'* [34] *But I tell you, Do not swear at all: either by heaven, for it is God's throne;* [35] *or by the earth, for it is his footstool; or by Jerusalem, for it is the city of the Great King.* [36] *And do not swear by your head, for you cannot make even one hair white or black.* [37] *Simply let your 'Yes' be 'Yes,' and your 'No,' 'No'; anything beyond this comes from the evil one."*

1. What is your initial reaction to this passage?
   - ❑ I think we're all in trouble.
   - ❑ It gets to the heart of the matter—our thoughts and attitudes.
   - ❑ Tell the American Bar Association about settling matters quickly out of court.
   - ❑ The part about gouging out your eye or cutting off your hand is pretty gross.
   - ❑ These high standards sure show us the necessity of grace.

2. What name did you really hate to be called when you were in grade school?
   - ❑ fatty / fatso
   - ❑ skinny / bean pole
   - ❑ dummy / idiot
   - ❑ egg head
   - ❑ I can't repeat it in polite company!
   - ❑ wimp
   - ❑ four-eyes
   - ❑ a racist name
   - ❑ other:_____

3. What did you do when you were called one of these names?
   - ❑ called them a name back
   - ❑ ignored it
   - ❑ told the teacher
   - ❑ slugged 'em
   - ❑ told my parents
   - ❑ got my friends to retaliate
   - ❑ cried
   - ❑ laughed it off

4. What was Jesus really saying in verses 21–22?
   - ❑ Anger is as bad as murder.
   - ❑ Your heart is as important as your behavior.
   - ❑ Name-callers will go to hell.
   - ❑ Actions get you in trouble with people; attitudes get you in trouble with God.
   - ❑ other:_____

5. Put an "X" on the line to indicate where you stand on each of these moral issues:

ON LAWSUITS:

Sue their socks off.	Only sue if you have to.	We can settle things if we just talk.

ON ADULTERY:

Hey, in today's world it's the norm.	Extramarital sex is a sin.	It is equally wrong to feast on sexual fantasy.

ON DIVORCE:

Divorce is a fact of life today.	Divorce is a last resort, a concession to our weakness.	Divorce is wrong in all circumstances.

"Each person is free to accept or reject Jesus. He can accept Jesus only to the degree that he accepts and lives by Jesus' moral teaching. A person can't accept Jesus as God and friend on the one hand and reject his moral teaching on the other."
—Richard Reichert

6. Why is it difficult for Christians to talk about sex in general, and lust in particular?
❒ because the subject is inappropriate
❒ because the subject is too personal
❒ because the subject is scary
❒ because the subject is embarrassing
❒ because the subject is associated with guilt and shame
❒ other:_____

7. What do you think Jesus would say about the way sexuality is portrayed in today's culture and media?
❒ He would be shocked.
❒ He would be glad to see how open and free people are.
❒ He would be appalled.
❒ He would be grieved.
❒ other:_____

8. The issue in the last part of this passage is not so much against taking oaths as it is a call for a character so full of integrity that others can trust our word without us having to resort to an oath. In which of the following areas is it easiest to keep your promises? Which is hardest?
❒ promises to my spouse   ❒ promises to my friends
❒ promises to my children   ❒ promises to myself
❒ promises to my boss   ❒ promises to God
❒ promises to other family members

9. Which of these moral demands challenges you the most?
❒ controlling my anger
❒ controlling my lust
❒ controlling my mouth—not swearing
❒ controlling my mouth—always telling the truth
❒ reconciling a broken relationship
❒ keeping my promises

COMMENT   Jesus' intent in the entire sermon is to demonstrate our desperate need for grace. He is not running a campaign to institute new laws. Instead, he shows his disciples common examples from life which revealed their lack of true, inner righteousness. His listeners then (and readers now) are all affected in some way by anger, hate, an unforgiving spirit, lust, divorce, lack of integrity, lack of generosity, and so forth. Jesus' point is that these common realities are symptoms of our brokenness and need for grace.

Romans 8:5–17 / Children of God

Read Romans 8:5–17 and share your responses to the following questions with your group. In this letter, Paul gives his most thorough explanation of what the life of faith is all about.

⁵Those who live according to the sinful nature have their minds set on what that nature desires; but those who live in accordance with the Spirit have their minds set on what the Spirit desires. ⁶The mind of sinful man is death, but the mind controlled by the Spirit is life and peace; ⁷the sinful mind is hostile to God. It does not submit to God's law, nor can it do so. ⁸Those controlled by the sinful nature cannot please God.

⁹You, however, are controlled not by the sinful nature but by the Spirit, if the Spirit of God lives in you. And if anyone does not have the Spirit of Christ, he does not belong to Christ. ¹⁰But if Christ is in you, your body is dead because of sin, yet your spirit is alive because of righteousness. ¹¹And if the Spirit of him who raised Jesus from the dead is living in you, he who raised Christ from the dead will also give life to your mortal bodies through his Spirit, who lives in you.

¹²Therefore, brothers, we have an obligation—but it is not to the sinful nature, to live according to it. ¹³For if you live according to the sinful nature, you will die; but if by the Spirit you put to death the misdeeds of the body, you will live, ¹⁴because those who are led by the Spirit of God are sons of God. ¹⁵For you did not receive a spirit that makes you a slave again to fear, but you received the Spirit of sonship. And by him we cry, "Abba, Father." ¹⁶The Spirit himself testifies with our spirit that we are God's children. ¹⁷Now if we are children, then we are heirs—heirs of God and co-heirs with Christ, if indeed we share in his sufferings in order that we may also share in his glory.

> "A lot of people say they love God with all their hearts, but then they stop there. He doesn't want just your heart; He wants your mind, your will, your emotions, every part of you."
> —Ron Luce

1. What did you have your mind "set on" in the seventh grade (e.g., schoolwork, sports, church and God, clothes, problems, the opposite sex, the future)?

2. In this passage, what does Paul say about the two options people have in living their lives? Where is the battle for the control of a person's life going to be fought—and won or lost?

3. What does Paul mean by a "sinful nature"? How are we to deal with it?

4. What does it mean to you that you are not God's slave, but his child?

5. If there was a pollution control device on your thought life right now, what would it register: Green—no problem? Orange—warning signs? Red—fire alert?

6. When unhealthy thoughts enter your mind, what have you found most useful in dealing with them?

7. What is God saying to you about morality?
   - ❏ I need to get my mind set on what the Spirit desires instead of what my sinful nature desires (v. 5).
   - ❏ I need to make sure I "belong to Christ" (v. 9).
   - ❏ I need to admit that I have a sinful nature (v. 12).
   - ❏ I need to let the Holy Spirit control my life (v. 13).
   - ❏ I need to deal with my fears (v. 15).
   - ❏ I need to accept my secure status as God's child (v. 16).

8. In verse 15 Paul says we can relate to God as "Abba"—which could be translated "Daddy." How intimate is your relationship with God? How does (or could) your closeness with God help you live a moral life?

Caring Time / 15–45 Minutes

Take time at the close to share any personal prayer requests. Answer the question:

"How can we help you in prayer this week?"

LEADER:
Ask the
group, "Who
are you going
to invite next
week?"

Then go around and let each person pray for the person on their right. Finish this sentence:

"Dear God, I want to speak to you about my friend _____."

During your prayer time, remember to pray for the empty chair and for the growth of your group.

Reference Notes

Summary. Scripture challenges how we view our position in life. Paul writes that we must not be enslaved to our sinful nature, as it leads to death. Although we are saved by grace (and do not have to live up to the Law), we need to seek the Spirit's guidance. As we change from the inside out, we view ourselves through God's eyes—as sons and daughters of God. If we set our minds on the things of God first—no matter the pressing circumstances of life around us—we will have the moral center to deal with difficulties. Also, we will gain a different view of one of the most crippling aspects of life—fear. From our new vantage point, fear is not that ominous. The Spirit of God leads us away from the spirit of fear—to a deeper understanding of our rightful place as children of God.

8:5 *live according to.* There are two options: to be preoccupied with sinful desires or to be focused on the desires of the Holy Spirit.

minds. Assumptions, values, outlook, desires, purpose—all that forms one's perspective on life. What a person thinks determines how one acts. One's conduct is guided by one's outlook.

8:6 *death / life.* These two opposite outlooks lead to two patterns of conduct which result in two spiritual states—death to God (because sin separates one from him) or life in the Spirit.

8:9 The distinguishing characteristic of the Christian is the indwelling of the Holy Spirit.

8:10–11 The consequence of having the Spirit within a person is life: life now (v. 10) and life eventually for the mortal body (v. 11), when the Christian experiences bodily resurrection.

8:12–13 Grammatically, it appears that Paul originally intended to complete the sentence by saying that not only do believers have no obligation to the flesh but that they do have an obligation to the Spirit to live according to it. Yet having stated the negative, he breaks off in mid-sentence to add the warning found in verse 13a. Once launched in this direction he balances off this statement in 13a by his assertion in verse 13b. But he then fails to complete the sentence begun in verse 12!

8:12 *obligation.* Christians have no further obligation to indulge their self-centeredness. Rather, they owe a debt to a life of holiness, i.e., they are obliged to live a life that is consistent with the life of the Spirit within them.

8:13 *put to death.* In Romans 7:4 Paul says that Christians have "died to the law" via Christ's once-for-all act of dying on the cross in their place. In response to this fact, believers are daily (the verb tense indicates an action that is repeated over and over) to "put to death" all those practices known to be wrong, all the attitudes that are not of God, and all the thoughts that would lead to sin. The presence of the Holy Spirit in one's life is not the end of the battle against sin but only the beginning, in the sense that now there is a hope of winning (see Matt. 16:24; Gal. 5:24).

you will live. That is, this is the evidence that one has truly come to Christ and thus has the promise of eternal life.

8:15 *spirit that makes you a slave.* The Holy Spirit brings one not into a new form of anxious bondage but rather unites one with Christ, enabling one to share his sonship.

you received. The verb tense indicates that this is a one-time, past action—something that happened at conversion.

sonship. The Roman practice of adoption was a most serious and complicated process, because a child was the absolute possession of his father (the father had the legal right to even kill his child). For a boy to be adopted into a new family, he was first symbolically "sold" by his father to the adopting father. Then the legal case for adoption was taken to the magistrate. The end result was that the child: (1) lost all rights in the old family while gaining full rights in the new one, (2) became a co-heir in his new father's estate, (3) had all his old debts canceled forever, and (4) became in all senses the child of the new father (Barclay).

cry. In the Psalms this word is used of urgent prayer (Ps. 3:4).

"Abba, Father." The very words that Jesus prayed in the Garden of Gethsemane (Mark 14:36).

Abba. An Aramaic word used by children; best translated "Daddy," signifying a close, intimate relationship.

8:16 In the Roman adoptive proceedings there were several witnesses to the ceremony who would, if a dispute arose later, verify that the particular child had actually been adopted. The Holy Spirit is the one who verifies a person's adoption into the family of God.

8:17 heirs. If someone is one of God's children, then that person is an heir, and will share in his riches. In fact, Jesus is God's true heir (Rom. 8:3), but since believers are "in Christ," they become sons and daughters of God by adoption (and so use the same words to address God as Jesus did), and thus are joint-heirs with Christ.

sufferings. This refers to "that element of suffering which is inseparable from faithfulness to Christ in a world which does not yet know him as Lord" (Cranfield). The willingness to suffer for Christ is a mark of belonging.

glory. Christians have the hope of sharing in the reign of Christ over all creation.

GROUP DIRECTORY

P.S.
If you have a new person in your group, be sure to add their name to the group directory inside the front cover.

Unconditional Love

3-PART AGENDA

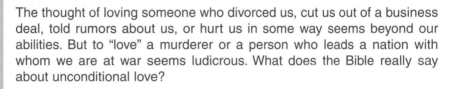

ICE-BREAKER
15 Minutes

BIBLE STUDY
30 Minutes

CARING TIME
15–45 Minutes

Will Rogers once said, "I never met a man I didn't like." Many of us would reply, "Evidently, Will never met so-and-so." If we are honest with ourselves, there are people in our lives with whom we can't get along and whom we don't like. However, we are taught in Scripture to love all people, including our enemies.

The thought of loving someone who divorced us, cut us out of a business deal, told rumors about us, or hurt us in some way seems beyond our abilities. But to "love" a murderer or a person who leads a nation with whom we are at war seems ludicrous. What does the Bible really say about unconditional love?

LEADER: If there are more than seven people at this meeting, divide into groups of 4 for Bible Study. Count off around the group: "one, two, one, two, etc."—and have the "ones" quickly move to another room. When you come back together for the Caring Time, have the group read about your Mission on page M5 of the center section.

In the Option 1 Study (from Matthew's Gospel), Jesus teaches us what it means to truly love our enemies. And in the Option 2 Study (from Paul's letter to the Philippians), we will discover Paul's teaching on unconditional love, which he learned in prison.

Remember the purpose of the Bible Study is to share your own story. Use this opportunity to deal with some issues in your life. Now, to get started, have fun doing the following ice-breaker.

Ice-Breaker / 15 Minutes

Bring Out Your Best! Use the questions below to share with the group what brings out your best ... and your worst! Go around the group on the first question. Then go around on the second question.

1. Finish this sentence: If you want to bring out my best, then ..."
   ❏ put me around playful people   ❏ give me lots of hugs
   ❏ compliment my appearance   ❏ give me a challenge
   ❏ put me in a competitive situation   ❏ feed me
   ❏ give me a charge card and send me to the mall

2. Finish this sentence: "If you want to bring out my worst ..."
   ❏ put me in a competitive situation   ❏ criticize me
   ❏ try putting me on a committee   ❏ try telling me what to do
   ❏ put me in a messy room   ❏ make me eat health food
   ❏ give me a charge card and send me to the mall

Bible Study / 30 Minutes

Option 1 / Gospel Study

Matthew 5:38–48 / Revenge and Love

Jesus totally rejects the thought of personal revenge, and calls instead for nonretaliation. Read Matthew 5:38–48 and discuss your responses to the following questions with your group.

38 "You have heard that it was said, 'Eye for eye, and tooth for tooth.' 39 But I tell you, Do not resist an evil person. If someone strikes you on the right cheek, turn to him the other also. 40 And if someone wants to sue you and take your tunic, let him have your cloak as well. 41 If someone forces you to go one mile, go with him two miles. 42 Give to the one who asks you, and do not turn away from the one who wants to borrow from you.

43 "You have heard that it was said, 'Love your neighbor and hate your enemy.' 44 But I tell you: Love your enemies and pray for those who persecute you, 45 that you may be sons of your Father in heaven. He causes his sun to rise on the evil and the good, and sends rain on the righteous and the unrighteous. 46 If you love those who love you, what reward will you get? Are not even the tax collectors doing that? 47 And if you greet only your brothers, what are you doing more than others? Do not even pagans do that? 48 Be perfect, therefore, as your heavenly Father is perfect."

1. Where would Jesus' words in this passage be the hardest to accept?
   ❏ at the local VFW
   ❏ at the local bank
   ❏ in an oppressed nation or people group
   ❏ in a persecuted church

"God's love for us is unconditional and this is the love we must have for others— Christian or non-Christian, friend or enemy. ... The moment we withhold our love for someone because of that person's words, actions, looks or personality— no matter how ugly or cruel he has been—we have placed a condition upon our love for that person."
—T. Max Melonuk

2. On the following moral issues, put an *"X"* on the line according to which position is closest to yours:

ON REVENGE:
Call in "Rambo."   Immediately forgive
                                                         and forget.

ON CRIME AND PUNISHMENT:
Call in "Dirty Harry."   Change lives through
                                                         love and opportunity.

ON WAR:
Call me a "hawk."   Call me a "dove."

3. How did your parents resolve conflicts between you and your brother, sister or friend?

❐ let us fight it out   ❐ sat us down to talk about it
❐ prayed about it   ❐ took sides
❐ yelled at us   ❐ sent us out of the house
❐ ignored it   ❐ They really didn't care.

4. When you get hurt in relationships now, what do you usually do?

❐ have it out with the person   ❐ sulk for three days
❐ withdraw into myself   ❐ talk to God
❐ cry on someone's shoulder   ❐ other:_____
❐ try to look at it from the other person's point of view

5. What have you found helpful in dealing with strained relationships?

❐ writing out my feelings   ❐ breaking off the relationship
❐ being up front with the person   ❐ other:_____
❐ doing something nice for them
❐ ignoring it and hoping for the best
❐ asking someone else to mediate

6. Which of these "enemies" would you have a hard time loving?

❐ anyone from the IRS   ❐ a rival at work
❐ my ex-spouse   ❐ conservatives
❐ my spouse's ex-spouse   ❐ liberals
❐ persons of a different race   ❐ other:_____
❐ those I fought in war

7. Think of someone who has hurt you in the past. What would your response be if they walked into the room right now?

❐ I would get up and leave.
❐ I would seek revenge—maybe even physical harm.
❐ I would remind them how they hurt me.
❐ I would forgive and forget.
❐ I would silently pray for them.
❐ It would depend upon their attitude toward me.

8. Where do you find it most difficult to "turn the other cheek"?

9. When you leave this meeting, how will you respond to the radical demands of this passage?
❐ conveniently forget it, like I've always done before
❐ struggle with it, but in the end stay with my relational patterns
❐ make some changes, but perhaps not all that this demands
❐ shoot for it all—turn my life around with unconditional love

Option 2 / Epistle Study

Phil. 1:12–18a,27–2:4 / Building Community

Paul wrote his letter to the Philippians from prison in Rome. Actually he wasn't in a jail—but was under house arrest. Paul was able to receive visitors and correspondence. He was, however, bound to a Roman guard by a short length of chain that ran from his wrist to the guard's wrist. It is not surprising that all the guards got to know Paul and his Gospel. Read Philippians 1:12–18a,27–2:4 and discuss your responses to the following questions with your group.

¹²Now I want you to know, brothers, that what has happened to me has really served to advance the gospel. ¹³As a result, it has become clear throughout the whole palace guard and to everyone else that I am in chains for Christ. ¹⁴Because of my chains, most of the brothers in the Lord have been encouraged to speak the word of God more courageously and fearlessly.

¹⁵It is true that some preach Christ out of envy and rivalry, but others out of goodwill. ¹⁶The latter do so in love, knowing that I am put here for the defense of the gospel. ¹⁷The former preach Christ out of selfish ambition, not sincerely, supposing that they can stir up trouble for me while I am in chains. ¹⁸But what does it matter? The important thing is that in every way, whether from false motives or true, Christ is preached. And because of this I rejoice. ...

²⁷Whatever happens, conduct yourselves in a manner worthy of the gospel of Christ. Then, whether I come and see you or only hear about you in my absence, I will know that you stand firm in one spirit, contending as one man for the faith of the gospel ²⁸without being frightened in any way by those who oppose you. This is a sign to them that they will be destroyed, but that you will be saved—and that by God. ²⁹For it has been granted to you on behalf of Christ not only to believe on him, but also to suffer for him, ³⁰since you are going through the same struggle you saw I had, and now hear that I still have.

2 *If you have any encouragement from being united with Christ, if any comfort from his love, if any fellowship with the Spirit, if any tender-*

ness and compassion, ²then make my joy complete by being like-minded, having the same love, being one in spirit and purpose. ³Do nothing out of selfish ambition or vain conceit, but in humility consider others better than yourselves. ⁴Each of you should look not only to your own interests, but also to the interests of others.

1. Are you the kind of person who sees the glass half-empty or half-full?

2. Although many were inspired to be bolder in proclaiming the Gospel by Paul's example, some used his imprisonment to advance their own honor, prestige or cause. How would you feel if that happened to you?

3. Paul was in prison but joyful. What trying circumstances are you dealing with? What is your attitude toward them?

4. What kind of struggles can a Christian expect (1:29–30)? What is the nearest you've come to suffering for Christ?

5. What kind of unity is Paul encouraging in 1:27 and 2:2? What kind of unity is important above all?

6. What is the closest you have come to being in a group that cared for one another like Paul describes in 2:1–4?

7. What does it mean to consider someone better than yourself (2:3)? How does humility differ from being a doormat?

8. Who do you admire because they truly put the interests of others ahead of their own interests?

9. Reflecting honestly, how much do you try to follow 2:3–4 in your daily life? How are you doing? How would you like to improve?

"Blessed are those who see the hand of God in the haphazard, inexplicable, and seemingly senseless circumstances of life."
—Erwin W. Lutzer

Caring Time / 15–45 Minutes

Take some time to share any personal prayer requests and answer the question:

"How do you need God's help in showing unconditional love to a difficult person in your life?"

LEADER:
Ask the group, "Who are you going to invite next week?"

Close with a short time of prayer, remembering the requests that have been shared. If you would like to pray in silence, say the word "Amen" when you have finished your prayer, so that the next person will know when to start.

Reference Notes

Summary. Paul reports on what has happened as a result of his imprisonment. He points to three positive outcomes, all involving the advance of the Gospel: (1) The Gospel is being noticed by all sorts of people who might otherwise not have heard it (v. 13); (2) the Christians in Rome have become bolder in their own proclamation (v. 14); and (3) even though some of the preaching that is going on springs from wrong motives, still the Gospel is getting out (vv. 15–18). Paul then shifts his focus from himself (and a report on his situation) to the Philippians (and advice on how to conduct themselves during the difficult times they are facing). Paul first exhorts the Philippians to be unified (1:27–30). Then he tells them that unity is achieved by means of self-sacrificing humility (2:1–4).

1:12 *brothers.* This is a generic term and means "brothers and sisters." By it Paul indicates the nature of his relationship with the Philippians. He and they are all part of one big family—God's family.

what has happened to me. This is literally, "my affairs," and refers to the circumstances of his imprisonment about which he says little.

1:13 *palace guard.* These men were the elite soldiers in the Roman army. They were the bodyguards of the emperor. Because Paul had been sent to Rome for a hearing before the emperor, they were given the task of guarding him. Paul's guards were changed every four hours or so; thus he got the chance to witness to a rotating coterie of soldiers from the key regiment in Rome. News of who he was and what he stood for apparently spread through the barracks and beyond into official circles.

for Christ. It had become clear to all involved that Paul was in prison not because he was a criminal who had been arrested for a crime he had committed or because he had dangerous political views. He was in jail simply because he was a Christian.

1:15 *envy and rivalry.* What motivates these people is some sort of grudge or hostility directed against Paul. They do not like him and want to hurt him by their preaching. What lay behind this animosity is not clear. Perhaps they looked on Paul in disdain because he was in jail, seeing this as a judgment from God against him. Or maybe they were jealous of Paul's role as an apostle and saw this as a golden opportunity to advance their own position and authority.

goodwill. Paul identifies the motives of the majority of the Christians. They preach out of a feeling of "benevolence" (v. 15) and "love" (v. 16).

1:18 *But what does it matter?* There is about Paul a truly astonishing, magnanimous spirit which does not care about personal reputation or who gets the credit as long as the job gets done. He does not vilify those who use their preaching as a pretext to attack him. He continues to think of them as "brothers." It is this spirit that enables Paul to cope, though in prison. He is not preoccupied with the misdeeds of these rivals. Instead, he rejoices over the fact that they preach Christ.

1:27 *in one spirit.* This is Paul's concern—their unity.

contending. This is another rare Greek word used in the New Testament only here and in Philippians 4:3. It is drawn from the world of sports and refers to athletes engaged in competition, striving together to achieve a common goal.

for the faith of the gospel. The goal to which Paul calls the Philippians is not victory on the battlefield or success in athletic competition, but preservation of the Christian faith.

1:28 *without being frightened.* Yet another rare word, used in the Bible only this one time. Its original reference was to horses that were timid and which shied easily. The Philippians must not let their opponents spook them into an uncontrolled stampede.

1:29 *has been granted.* It seems to be an assumption on Paul's part, expressed both here and elsewhere, that Christians will suffer (see for example, 1 Thess. 3:3–4). Yet Paul does not view suffering as something one has to put up with reluctantly. In fact, as Paul indicates here, suffering for the sake of Christ is a gift of grace. (The verb "has been granted" is derived from the same root as the Greek word for "grace.")

1:30 *the same struggle.* Paul alludes to two incidents of persecution known by the Philippians: the one in Philippi on his first visit (Acts 16:16–40) and the other in Jerusalem that resulted in his present imprisonment (Acts 21:27–26:32). In each instance Paul's struggle was with those who were opposed to his Christian beliefs and practices. In both cases his opponents stirred up the crowds against him and forced the Roman authorities to take him into custody. It is important to note that Paul was not being persecuted by Rome. His persecution originated with opponents of the Gospel. The Philippians are also facing the same opponents.

2:1 By means of four clauses, Paul urges the Philippians to say "yes" to his request that they live together in harmony. They have strong incentive to be united to one another, he says, because of their experience of the love, fellowship, mercy and compassion of God the Father, Son and Holy Spirit.

if. In Greek, this construction assumes a positive response, e.g., "If you have any encouragement, as of course you do ... ."

2:2 *like-minded.* This is literally, "think the same way." However, by this phrase what Paul is encouraging is not simple conformity of ideas and opinions. The Greek word for "think" is more comprehensive and involves not only one's mind but one's feelings, attitudes and will. Paul is calling for a far deeper form of unity than simple doctrinal conformity.

2:3 *selfish ambition.* This means working to advance oneself without thought for others.

vain conceit. This is the only occurrence of this word in the New Testament. Literally, it means "vain glory" (*kenodoxia*) which is asserting oneself over God who alone is worthy of true glory (*doxa*). People who are characterized by this attitude arrogantly assert that they are right even though what they hold is false. These are people who are concerned about personal prestige.

humility. This was not a virtue that was valued by the Greeks in the first century. They considered this to be the attitude of a slave, i.e., servility. In the Old Testament this was understood to be the proper attitude to hold before God. What Paul means by humility is defined by the phrase that follows. Humility is "considering others better than yourself." Christians are to accord others the same dignity and respect that Christ has given to all people. Humility involves seeing others not on the basis of how clever, attractive or pious they are, but through the eyes of Christ who died for them.

2:4 *look not only to your own interests.* This means "keeping your eye on" your own interests. Preoccupation with personal interests, along with "selfish ambition" and "vain conceit" make unity impossible. Individualism and partisanship work against community. Note that Paul says "look *not only* to your own interests." Personal interests are important (although not to the exclusion of everything else). This is a call to love, not to masochism.

the interests of others. The Philippians should focus on the good points in others. "Rejoice in the honor paid to others rather than to that paid to yourself" (Bruce). See also Romans 15:1–3 and Galatians 6:2.

SESSION

4

Spirituality

3-PART AGENDA

ICE-BREAKER
15 Minutes

BIBLE STUDY
30 Minutes

CARING TIME
15–45 Minutes

In recent years, interest in spirituality has increased. Within Christianity, there has been a renewed interest in the ministry of the Holy Spirit and in the practice of spiritual disciplines. In our society, there also has been growth in the area of Eastern religions, the occult and the New Age movement.

However, this attraction to spirituality is nothing new. People have always been in search of a "higher power." Centuries ago, Augustine wrote, "There is a God-shaped vacuum in every person that only Christ can fill." Today, people are still trying to fill that vacuum—but often apart from Christ. True spirituality comes through participating in spiritual disciplines.

LEADER: If you have a new person at this session, remember to use Option 1 rather than Option 2 for the Bible Study. During the Caring Time, don't forget to keep praying for the empty chair.

"Discipline" is not a word which we enjoy. Discipline involves setting goals, and following steps to achieve those goals. The word "self" is key. Self-discipline is part of kingdom living and part of the Christian life to which we are called.

In the following studies, we will see that Scripture views spirituality as more than religious activities. In the Option 1 Study (from Matthew's Gospel), Jesus teaches about religious activities and the proper motives for these activities. In the Option 2 Study (from Galatians), Paul discusses spiritual maturity and the importance of producing spiritual fruit in our lives.

Ice-Breaker / 15 Minutes

Connected With the Creator. Let one person start out by answering two of the questions below—in any order. Then ask another person to share, etc. around the group.

1. Describe a spot in nature that was special to you when you were a child.

2. To which of the following scenes from nature would you go if you wanted to feel close to God?
   - ❐ the ocean
   - ❐ a forest
   - ❐ a waterfall
   - ❐ a sunny day
   - ❐ a mountain
   - ❐ a mountain stream
   - ❐ a thunderstorm
   - ❐ other:_____

3. Psalm 89:11 states, "The heavens are yours, and yours also the earth; you founded the world and all that is in it." Which of the following aspects of God's creation do you desire to draw from?
   - ❐ the ocean—In my "low tides" I want to believe in "high tides."
   - ❐ a mountain—I need to feel that some things are constant and unmovable.
   - ❐ a mountain stream—I need to feel peace in the midst of the rush.
   - ❐ a forest—I need to feel part of a community of life.
   - ❐ a waterfall—I need to feel God's power in my life.
   - ❐ a thunderstorm—I need to let loose the turmoil I feel inside.
   - ❐ a sunny day—I need to feel warm and invigorated.

Bible Study / 30 Minutes

Option 1 / Gospel Study

Matthew 6:1–18 / Give, Pray, Fast

Jesus discusses how the righteousness he calls for relates to three examples of common Jewish piety: almsgiving, prayer and fasting. Read Matthew 6:1–18 and discuss your responses to the following questions with your group.

6 *"Be careful not to do your 'acts of righteousness' before men, to be seen by them. If you do, you will have no reward from your Father in heaven.*

²"So when you give to the needy, do not announce it with trumpets, as the hypocrites do in the synagogues and on the streets, to be honored by men. I tell you the truth, they have received their reward in full. ³But when you give to the needy, do not let your left hand know what your right hand is doing, ⁴so that your giving may be in secret. Then your Father, who sees what is done in secret, will reward you.

⁵"And when you pray, do not be like the hypocrites, for they love to pray standing in the synagogues and on the street corners to be seen by men. I tell you the truth, they have received their reward in full. ⁶But when you pray, go into your room, close the door and pray to your Father, who is unseen. Then your Father, who sees what is done in secret, will reward you. ⁷And when you pray, do not keep on babbling like pagans, for they think they will be heard because of their many words. ⁸Do not be like them, for your Father knows what you need before you ask him.

⁹"This, then, is how you should pray:

" 'Our Father in heaven,
hallowed be your name,
¹⁰your kingdom come,
your will be done
    on earth as it is in heaven.
¹¹Give us today our daily bread.
¹²Forgive us our debts,
    as we also have forgiven our debtors.
¹³And lead us not into temptation,
but deliver us from the evil one.'

¹⁴For if you forgive men when they sin against you, your heavenly Father will also forgive you. ¹⁵But if you do not forgive men their sins, your Father will not forgive your sins.

¹⁶"When you fast, do not look somber as the hypocrites do, for they disfigure their faces to show men they are fasting. I tell you the truth, they have received their reward in full. ¹⁷But when you fast, put oil on your head and wash your face, ¹⁸so that it will not be obvious to men that you are fasting, but only to your Father, who is unseen; and your Father, who sees what is done in secret, will reward you."

1. Which of these phrases describes your first reaction to Jesus' words in this passage?
   ❑ What good is it to do good if you don't get credit for it?
   ❑ Preachers should pay attention to the part about not needing "many words"!
   ❑ This is impractical—people need some credit for giving: getting their name on a list or a plaque or something.
   ❑ Jesus is right—our religious practices should be for God, not people.

2. In your home, how openly is the Christian faith expressed (in practices like giving, praying, worshiping, fasting, etc.)?
   ❑ We're very expressive, and want the whole world to know it.
   ❑ We're pretty expressive, but don't make a lot of noise about it.
   ❑ We're not outwardly expressive, but our faith is really sincere.
   ❑ We're rather private when it comes to these things.
   ❑ Who gave you the right to ask such a personal question?!
   ❑ Members of my family differ so much, that it's hard to explain.
   ❑ other:_____

" Every
Christian
needs a half
hour of prayer
each day,
except when
he is busy,
then he needs
an hour."
—Saint
Francis of
Sales

3. If you could change your answer to the last question, how would you like to be able to answer the question?

4. Rate yourself on the scale below for each form of spiritual discipline:

PRAYER:

1	2	3	4	5	6	7	8	9	10

I never think of doing this.   This is an important part
of my spiritual life.

SCRIPTURE READING / MEDITATION:

1	2	3	4	5	6	7	8	9	10

I never think of doing this.   This is an important part
of my spiritual life.

ACTS OF GIVING / CHARITY:

1	2	3	4	5	6	7	8	9	10

I never think of doing this.   This is an important part
of my spiritual life.

FASTING:

1	2	3	4	5	6	7	8	9	10

I never think of doing this.   This is an important part
of my spiritual life.

5. Who is an example to you of a person whose daily life is molded by the spiritual disciplines Jesus taught in this passage? What could you do to be more like that person?

6. What do you need to change in your life to apply Jesus' principle of giving in a proper way to the needy?
    ❐ I need a motivation check.
    ❐ I need to find more ways to give.
    ❐ I need to be more secretive about my giving.
    ❐ I need to give more.
    ❐ other: _____

7. The most difficult part of my prayer life is:
    ❐ getting around to it
    ❐ accepting God's answers
    ❐ knowing how to pray and what to say
    ❐ living each moment as prayer
    ❐ being motivated to pray
    ❐ believing that prayer can really make a difference
    ❐ praying out loud in public
    ❐ listening for God's voice
    ❐ forgiving the sins of others against me
    ❐ knowing that my heavenly Father really does know my needs
    ❐ other: _____

ENDIPITY

101

Game Plan

Leadership
Training
Supplement

YOU ARE
HERE

BIRTH   GROWTH   RELEASE

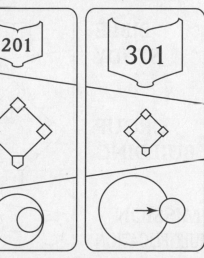

What is the game plan for your group in the 101 stage?

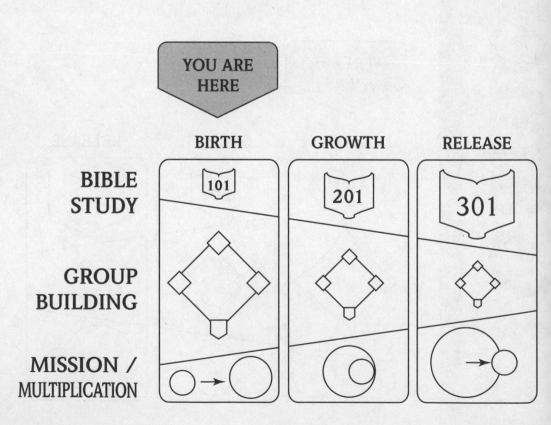

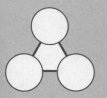

e 3-Legged Stool

The three essentials in a healthy small group are Bible Study, Group Building and Mission / Multiplication. You need all three to stay balanced—like a 3-legged stool.
  • To focus only on Bible Study will lead to scholasticism.
  • To focus only on Group Building will lead to narcissism.
  • To focus only on Mission will lead to burnout.
You need a game plan for the life cycle of the group where all three of these elements are present in a mission-driven strategy. In the first stage of the group, here is the game plan.

Bible Study

To share your spiritual story through Scripture.

The greatest gift you can give a group is the gift of your spiritual story—the story of your spiritual beginnings, your spiritual growing pains, struggles, hopes and fears. The Bible Study is designed to help you tell your spiritual story to the group.

Group Building

To become a caring community.

In the first stage of a group, note how the baseball diamond is larger than the book and the circles. This is because Group Building is the priority in the first stage. Group Building is a four-step process to become a close-knit group. Using the baseball diamond illustration, the goal of Group Building—bonding—is home plate. But to get there you have to go around the bases.

Mission / Multiplication

To grow your group numerically and spiritually.

The mission of your group is the greatest mission anyone can give their life to—to bring new people into a personal relationship with Christ and the fellowship of a Christian community. This purpose will become more prominent in the second and third stages of your group. In this stage, the goal is to invite new people into your group and try to double.

Leadership Training

Bible Study

In the first stage of a group, the Bible Study is where you get to know each other and share your spiritual stories. The Bible Study is designed to give the leader the option of going LIGHT or HEAVY, depending on the background of the people in the group. TRACK 1 is especially designed for beginner groups who do not know a lot about the Bible or each other. TRACK 2 is for groups who are familiar with the Bible and with one another.

Track 1 — Relational Bible Study (Stories)

Designed around a guided questionnaire, the questions move across the Disclosure Scale from "no risk" questions about people in the Bible story to "high risk" questions about your own life and how you would react in that situation. "If you had been in the story ..." or "the person in the story like me is ... ." The questions are open-ended—with multiple-choice options and no right or wrong answers. A person with no background knowledge of the Bible may actually have the advantage because the questions are based on first impressions.

The STORY in Scripture	GUIDED QUESTIONNAIRE 1 2 3 4 5 6 7 8	My STORY compared

TRACK 1: Light RELATIONAL BIBLE STUDY	TRACK 2: Heavy INDUCTIVE BIBLE STUDY
• Based on Bible stories • Open-ended questions • To share your spiritual story	• Based on Bible teachings • With observation questions • To dig into Scripture

Track 2 — Inductive Bible Study (Teachings)

For groups who know each other, TRACK 2 gives you the option to go deeper in Bible Study, with questions about the text on three levels:

- Observation: What is the text saying?
- Interpretation: What does it mean?
- Application: What are you going to do about it?

M4

Group Building

The Baseball Diamond illustrates the four-step sharing process in bonding to become a group: (1) input; (2) feedback; (3) deeper input; and (4) deeper feedback. This process is carefully structured into the seven sessions of this course, as follows:

 Sharing My Story. My religious background. My early years and where I am right now in my spiritual journey.

 Affirming Each Other's Story. "Thank you for sharing ..." "Your story became a gift to me ..." "Your story helps me to understand where you are coming from ..."

 Sharing My Needs. "This is where I'm struggling and hurting. This is where I need to go—what I need to do."

 Caring for One Another. "How can we help you in prayer this week?" Ministry occurs as the group members serve one another through the Holy Spirit.

Mission / Multiplication

To prove that your group is "Mission-Driven," now is the time to start praying for your new "baby"—a new group to be born in the future. This is the MISSION of your group.

The birthing process begins by growing your group to about 10 or 12 people. Here are three suggestions to help your group stay focused on your Mission:

1. **Empty Chair.** Pull up an empty chair at the Caring Time and ask God to fill this chair at the next meeting.

2. **Refrigerator List.** Jot down the names of people you are going to invite and put this list on the refrigerator.

3. **New Member Home.** Move to the home of the newest member—where their friends will feel comfortable when they come to the group. On the next page, some of your questions about bringing new people into your group are answered.

What if a new person joins the group in the third or fourth session?

Call the "Option Play" and go back to an EASY Bible Study that allows this person to "share their story" and get to know the people in the group.

What do you do when the group gets too large for sharing?

Take advantage of the three-part agenda and subdivide into groups of four for the Bible Study time. Count off around the group: "one, two, one, two"—and have the "ones" move quickly to another room for sharing.

What is the long-term expectation of the group for mission?

To grow the size of the group and eventually start a new group after one or two years.

What do you do when the group does not want to multiply?

This is the reason why this MISSION needs to be discussed at the beginning of a group—not at the end. If the group is committed to this MISSION at the outset, and works on this mission in stage one, they will be ready for multiplication at the end of the final stage.

What are the principles behind the Serendipity approach to Bible Study for a beginner group?

1. *Level the Playing Field.* Start the sharing with things that are easy to talk about and where everyone is equal—things that are instantly recallable—light, mischieviously revealing and childlike. Meet at the human side before moving into spiritual things.

2. *Share Your Spiritual Story.* Group Building, especially for new groups, is essential. It is crucial for Bible Study in beginner groups to help the group become a community by giving everyone the opportunity to share their spiritual history.

3. *Open Questions / Right Brain.* Open-ended questions are better than closed questions. Open questions allow for options, observations and a variety of opinions in which no one is right or wrong. Similarly, "right-brained" questions are

better than "left-brained" questions. Right-brained questions seek out your first impressions, tone, motives and subjective feelings about the text. Right-brained questions work well with narratives. Multiple-choice questionnaires encourage people who know very little about the Bible. Given a set of multiple-choice options, a new believer is not threatened, and a shy person is not intimidated. Everyone has something to contribute.

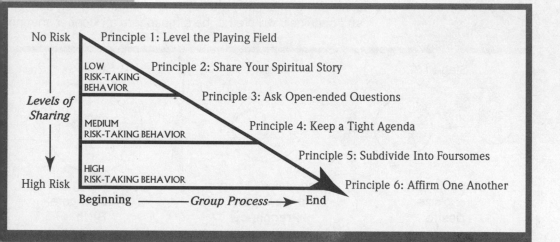

Levels of Sharing

No Risk — Principle 1: Level the Playing Field

LOW RISK-TAKING BEHAVIOR — Principle 2: Share Your Spiritual Story

Principle 3: Ask Open-ended Questions

MEDIUM RISK-TAKING BEHAVIOR — Principle 4: Keep a Tight Agenda

Principle 5: Subdivide Into Foursomes

HIGH RISK-TAKING BEHAVIOR — Principle 6: Affirm One Another

High Risk

Beginning ——— *Group Process* ➔ End

4. Tight Agenda. A tight agenda is better than a loose agenda for beginning small groups. Those people who might be nervous about "sharing" will find comfort knowing that the meeting agenda has been carefully organized. The more structure the first few meetings have the better, especially for a new group. Some people are afraid that a structured agenda will limit discussion. In fact, the opposite is true. The Serendipity agenda is designed to keep the discussion focused on what's important and to bring out genuine feelings, issues, and areas of need. If the goal is to move the group toward deeper relationships and a deeper experience of God, then a structured agenda is the best way to achieve that goal.

5. Fearless Foursomes. Dividing your small group into foursomes during the Bible Study can be a good idea. In groups of four, everyone will have an opportunity to participate and you can finish the Bible Study in 30 minutes. In groups of eight or more, the Bible Study will need to be longer and you will take away from the Caring Time.

Also, by subdividing into groups of four for the Bible Study time, you give others a chance to develop their skills at leading a group—in preparation for the day when you develop a small cell to eventually move out and birth a new group.

6. *Affirm the person and their story.* Give positive feedback to group members: "Thank you for sharing ... your story really helps me to understand where you are coming from ... your story was a real gift to me ... " This affirmation given honestly and genuinely will create the atmosphere for deeper sharing.

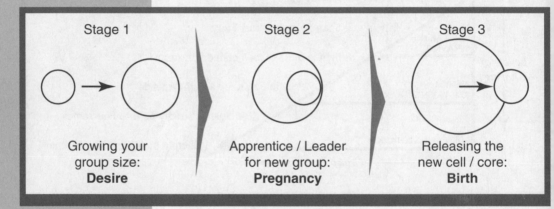

Stage 1	Stage 2	Stage 3
Growing your group size: **Desire**	Apprentice / Leader for new group: **Pregnancy**	Releasing the new cell / core: **Birth**

What is the next stage of our group all about?

In the next stage, the 201 BIBLE STUDY is deeper, GROUP BUILDING focuses on developing your gifts, and in the MISSION you will identify an Apprentice / Leader and two others within your group who will eventually become the leadership core of a new group down the road a bit.

8. Which part of what is known as the Lord's Prayer (vv. 9–13) is the most difficult for you to pray with sincerity.
   - ❐ "Our Father"—It conjures up negative memories and images of my father.
   - ❐ "hallowed be your name"—It's not easy for me to give God uninhibited praise.
   - ❐ "your kingdom come"—I like life the way it is, and am not particularly looking forward to God's kingdom on this earth.
   - ❐ "your will be done"—I prefer my will, thank you very much.
   - ❐ "Give us today our daily bread"—It is hard for me to depend on God for my daily needs.
   - ❐ "Forgive us our debts"—No one likes to admit their sins.
   - ❐ "Forgive us ... as we also have forgiven our debtors"—There is a person I really don't want to forgive.
   - ❐ "lead us not into temptation"—Quite frankly, I like to indulge in some temptations on occasion.
   - ❐ "deliver us from evil"—I want to be delivered from some evil things, but not all of them.

9. If I am going to get serious about my spiritual life, I need to:
   - ❐ set time aside daily for devotions
   - ❐ learn how to listen for God's voice
   - ❐ be committed to a group like this
   - ❐ rearrange my priorities
   - ❐ get involved in giving to others
   - ❐ other:_____

COMMENT Jesus makes it clear that his followers are not to make a public display of religious devotion. There is a radical realignment in the hearts of those who pray with sincerity, in God's name, and for his kingdom and will. Outward actions mean very little unless our heart, motives and inner attitude are all pure. Spiritual disciplines are not easy. We can always think of 10 other things we should be doing. But we need to follow our spiritual and moral compass and say no to other things, so that we can put first things first.

Option 2 / Epistle Study

Galatians 5:16–26 / Living by the Spirit

Read Galatians 5:16–26 and discuss your responses to the following questions with your group.

¹⁶So I say, live by the Spirit, and you will not gratify the desires of the sinful nature. ¹⁷For the sinful nature desires what is contrary to the Spirit, and the Spirit what is contrary to the sinful nature. They are in conflict with each other, so that you do not do what you want. ¹⁸But if you are led by the Spirit, you are not under law.

¹⁹The acts of the sinful nature are obvious: sexual immorality, impurity and debauchery; ²⁰idolatry and witchcraft; hatred, discord, jealousy, fits of rage, selfish ambition, dissensions, factions ²¹and envy; drunkenness, orgies, and the like. I warn you, as I did before, that those who live like this will not inherit the kingdom of God.

²²But the fruit of the Spirit is love, joy, peace, patience, kindness, goodness, faithfulness, ²³gentleness and self-control. Against such things there is no law. ²⁴Those who belong to Christ Jesus have crucified the sinful nature with its passions and desires. ²⁵Since we live by the Spirit, let us keep in step with the Spirit. ²⁶Let us not become conceited, provoking and envying each other.

1. On a scale of 0 (none) to 10 (tons), how many "wild oats" did you sow in your youth?

2. In this letter, Paul has repeatedly warned the Galatians about being enslaved to legalism. What does he warn them about being enslaved to in this passage?

3. If we are made alive by the Spirit, why do we still struggle with sin?

4. Since we are not under the Old Testament Law, what is wrong with indulging in our sinful nature once in a while?

5. Can a person who lives according to the "acts of the sinful nature" in verses 19–21 be a true Christian (see notes on v. 21)?

6. What is the biggest change that being a Christian has made in your life?

7. How can you and God's Spirit weed out the sinful nature and grow the fruit of the Spirit (see note on v. 24)?

8. Which of the fruit of the Spirit (vv. 22–23) are blossoming in your life right now? Which are still in the bud?

9. Comparing your life to a fruit tree, are you feeling: Young and green but growing? Healthy and productive? Full of wild branches that need pruning? Worn out and drained of life?

"The fruits of the Spirit are nothing but the virtues of Christ."
—Friedrich Schleiermacher

Caring Time / 15–45 Minutes

LEADER:
Ask the group, "Who are you going to invite next week?"

During your time of prayer, remember the people who shared and what they said. If you don't know how to begin, finish this sentence:

"Lord, I want to talk with you about my friend ..."

Don't forget to keep praying for the empty chair and inviting people to your group.

When your group is finished praying, close with the Lord's Prayer—from the wording of the New International Version.

"Our Father
in heaven,
hallowed be your name,
your kingdom come,
your will be done
on earth as it is in heaven.
Give us today our daily bread.
Forgive us our debts,
as we also have forgiven our debtors.
And lead us not into temptation,
but deliver us from the evil one.
For yours is the kingdom and the power
and the glory forever. Amen."

Reference Notes

Summary. Having warned against losing one's freedom by submitting to circumcision (Gal. 5:1–2), Paul now warns about losing freedom by submitting to sinful desires.

5:16 *live by the Spirit.* Literally, "walk by the Spirit"; i.e., let the way you live, your conduct, be directed by the Holy Spirit. It is the Holy Spirit, not the Law, who will bring about a moral lifestyle.

5:17 Two principles are at war in the Christian's life. "But the believer is not the helpless battle ground of two opposing forces. If he yields to the flesh, he is enslaved by it, but if he obeys the prompting of the Spirit, he is liberated" (Bruce).

5:18 The Spirit is as opposed to the Law as to the sinful nature (vv. 16–17). To be led by the Spirit enables a person to resist sinful desire. To be under Law, however, gives a person no protection at all against such inner cravings.

5:19 *acts of the sinful nature.* To illustrate specifically the sort of lifestyle that emerges when the sinful nature is allowed its way, Paul produces a representative list of vices.

5:20 *idolatry.* The worship of any idol, be it a carved image of God (a statue) or an abstract substitute for God (a status symbol). An idol is identified as such because when faced with a choice, a person will follow its leading. Money, for example, becomes an idol when to gain it a person will do anything.

witchcraft. *Pharmakeia* is literally "the use of drugs," which was often associated with the practice of sorcery.

hatred. This is the underlying political, social and religious hostility which drives individuals and communities apart.

discord. This is the type of contention which leads to factions.

selfish ambition. This word came to refer to anyone who worked only for his or her own good and not for the benefit of others.

factions. This means the party spirit which leads people to regard those with whom they disagree as enemies.

5:21 *drunkenness.* In the first century, diluted wine was drunk regularly by all ages, but drunkenness was not common and was condemned (because it was thought to turn a person into a beast).

and the like. The list is representative, not exhaustive—touching, in order, upon the sins of sensuality, idolatry, social dissension, and intemperance.

not inherit. The issue here is not sins into which one falls, but sin as a lifestyle. These are evidence of a life not controlled by the Spirit, and therefore the implication is that such a person has not been born from above and become a child of God.

5:22 *fruit of the Spirit.* These are the traits which characterize the child of God. Again, the list is representative and not exhaustive.

love. *Agape;* in contrast, there is *eros* (sexual love), *philos* (warm feeling to friends and family), and *storge* (family affection). None of these adequately describe the self-giving, active benevolence that is meant to characterize Christian love, hence the repeated use in the New Testament of *agape*—a relatively uncommon word redefined by Christians to bear this meaning.

joy. The Greek word is *chara*, and comes from the same root as "grace" (*charis*). It is not based on earthly things or human achievement; it is a gift from God based on a right relationship with him.

peace. The prime meaning of this word is not negative ("an absence of conflict"), but positive ("the presence of that which brings wholeness and well-being").

patience. This is the ability to be steadfast with people, refusing to give up on them.

kindness. This is the compassionate use of strength for the good of another.

goodness. This implies moral purity which reflects the character of God.

faithfulness. This is to be reliable and trustworthy.

5:23 gentleness. According to Aristotle, this is the virtue that lies between excessive proneness to anger and the inability to be angry; it implies control of oneself.

self-control. This is control of one's sensual passions, rather than control of one's anger (as in gentleness).

there is no law. While it is possible to legislate certain forms of behavior, one cannot command love, joy, peace, etc. These are each gifts of God's grace. With this list of qualities one moves into a whole new realm of reality, well beyond the sphere of Law.

5:24 have crucified the sinful nature. It is via the Cross that a person dies to the power of the Law (Gal. 2:19). Paul indicates here that in the same way, a person also dies to the power of their sinful nature. The verb indicates that this is not something done *to* the Christian but *by* the Christian. The Christian actively and deliberately has repented of (turned away from) the old wayward patterns of life.

5:25 live by the Spirit. In the same way that the death of the ego (the "I" principle) is replaced by the mind of Christ (Gal. 2:20), here Paul indicates that the death of the sinful nature is replaced by the life of the Spirit.

let us. Having just indicated that the Christian does live by the power of the Spirit, Paul (in characteristic fashion) balances off that indicative ("this is the way things are") with an imperative ("now you do this"). "Walking by the Spirit is the outward manifestation, in action and speech, of living by the Spirit. Living by the Spirit is the root; walking by the Spirit is the fruit and that fruit is nothing less than the practical reproduction of the character (and therefore conduct) of Christ in the lives of his people" (Bruce).

SESSION

5

Contentment

3-PART AGENDA

ICE-BREAKER
15 Minutes

BIBLE STUDY
30 Minutes

CARING TIME
15–45 Minutes

We need to set our moral and spiritual compass with the end of life in mind. This means that you start with the image of what you want at the end of your life. This picture serves as your paradigm through which everything else in your life is filtered. Each part of your life (and each day's behavior) is examined in the context of the whole—what really matters the most to you.

What do you want to accomplish with your life? What is the most impor tant thing to you? How will you reach your goals? We live in a cultur which tells us that our goals should include the accumulation of things material wealth, power and prestige. Our world tells us to strive for more but Jesus speaks of being content with what we have in this world. It i difficult to be satisfied with what we have—we always want somethin more.

Jesus reminds us that accumulating wealth or possessions as a mean of obtaining security in life is incompatible with seeking God's kingdom We know that we should be content with what we have in life. We kno that we shouldn't worr about tomorrow or th future. But how can we b content when we have s many concerns in our life We know that worry sap our time and energ Besides, 90 percent c

LEADER: If you haven't already, now is the time to start thinking about the next step for your group. Take a look at the 201 courses (the second stage in the small group life cycle) on the inside of the back cover.

what we worry about never happens. What can we do to increase cor tentment and decrease worry?

In the Option 1 Study (from Matthew's Gospel), we see Jesus' respons to worry. In the passage, Jesus puts worry in the right perspective. In th Option 2 Study (from Paul's first letter to Timothy), we learn that worry not a requirement of life.

Ice-Breaker / 15 Minutes

I Dream of Genie. If you could have three wishes, which three would you choose from the list below?

☐ WIN THE LOTTERY: never have to work again

☐ SECURE JOB: lifetime guarantee with benefits

☐ PERFECT BODY: appearance that stands out in a crowd

☐ STRESS-FREE LIFE: no pain, no struggle, no tension

☐ CLOSE FAMILY: no hassles, lots of love and support

☐ GOOD HEALTH: long life, full of vigor and vitality

☐ ONE DEEP, ABIDING FRIENDSHIP: someone who will always be there

☐ SUCCESS: fame and recognition in your chosen field

☐ STRONG, SPIRITUAL FAITH: a deep, satisfying relationship with God

☐ OTHER: _____

Bible Study / 30 Minutes

Option 1 / Gospel Study

Matthew 6:19–34 / Not to Worry

The previous section (6:1–18) concentrated on how true righteousness differs from the self-serving legalism of the Pharisees. Here the emphasis is on how this righteousness differs from the self-absorbed materialism of the Gentiles. Discipleship to Jesus means that the believer must choose between two treasures (19–21), two visions (22–23), two masters (24), and two attitudes (25–34). Read Matthew 6:19–34 and discuss your responses to the following questions with your group.

[19]*"Do not store up for yourselves treasures on earth, where moth and rust destroy, and where thieves break in and steal.* [20]*But store up for yourselves treasures in heaven, where moth and rust do not destroy, and where thieves do not break in and steal.* [21]*For where your treasure is, there your heart will be also.*

[22]*"The eye is the lamp of the body. If your eyes are good, your whole body will be full of light.* [23]*But if your eyes are bad, your whole body will be full of darkness. If then the light within you is darkness, how great is that darkness!*

²⁴"No one can serve two masters. Either he will hate the one and love the other, or he will be devoted to the one and despise the other. You cannot serve both God and Money.

²⁵"Therefore I tell you, do not worry about your life, what you will eat or drink; or about your body, what you will wear. Is not life more important than food, and the body more important than clothes? ²⁶Look at the birds of the air; they do not sow or reap or store away in barns, and yet your heavenly Father feeds them. Are you not much more valuable than they? ²⁷Who of you by worrying can add a single hour to his life?

²⁸"And why do you worry about clothes? See how the lilies of the field grow. They do not labor or spin. ²⁹Yet I tell you that not even Solomon in all his splendor was dressed like one of these. ³⁰If that is how God clothes the grass of the field, which is here today and tomorrow is thrown into the fire, will he not much more clothe you, O you of little faith? ³¹So do not worry, saying, 'What shall we eat?' or 'What shall we drink?' or 'What shall we wear?' ³²For the pagans run after all these things, and your heavenly Father knows that you need them. ³³But seek first his kingdom and his righteousness, and all these things will be given to you as well. ³⁴Therefore do not worry about tomorrow, for tomorrow will worry about itself. Each day has enough trouble of its own."

1. If you had heard this passage for the first time (and did not know that Jesus said it), what would your first reaction have been?
❒ Sounds like a hippie from the '60s.
❒ This person is out of touch with the real world.
❒ This guy doesn't have to support a family.
❒ I wish it were that easy.
❒ Sounds good, but I'm not sure I have what it takes to do it.
❒ This is the needed prescription for our high-pressure world.

2. If you could choose to live a simple life (like the Waltons on Walton's Mountain) with few amenities and fewer debts, would you do it?

3. When Jesus said, "Do not worry about your life," he meant:
❒ Don't sweat the small stuff.
❒ Live one day at a time.
❒ Don't plan for tomorrow.
❒ Plan ahead so you don't worry.
❒ Trusting God is an important part of planning for tomorrow.
❒ God will take care of us, no matter what we do.
❒ Worry is a waste of time and energy.
❒ Depend on God for things you can't control.

"Materialism is more than just our tendency to buy more than we should. It's our tendency to buy a false world view which places material things at the center of life."
—James Paternoster

4. What did Jesus mean when he said, "But seek first his kingdom and his righteousness, and all these things will be given to you as well" (v. 33)?
❏ If you follow Jesus, he will make sure you get all the things you want.
❏ If you do what God wants, God will help you with your basic needs.
❏ If you learn to love Jesus, it won't matter whether you have those other things.
❏ If you trust God, he will take care of you.
❏ other:_____

5. Jesus' teaching presents a different perspective than our culture's, which measures a person's worth by his or her wealth. What pressures have tried to convince you to serve money?
❏ advertisements / media
❏ employer pressure to work overtime
❏ peer pressure to create a certain image
❏ jealousy over someone else's possessions
❏ other:_____

6. How content are you in each of the following areas of your life? Write the percent of your contentment on the lines below to indicate where you are—somewhere between 0% contentment (Panic Button) and 100% contentment (No Problem) for each category:
___ my family   ___ my job / career
___ my self-worth   ___ my relationship with friends
___ my relationship with God   ___ my health
___ my finances   ___ the future

7. If Jesus were to analyze your life, what do you think he would say your "treasure" is?
❏ my plans for the future   ❏ my reputation
❏ my desire for pleasure   ❏ my relationship with him
❏ my money and possessions   ❏ other:_____
❏ my desire to serve others
❏ my desire for more money and possessions

8. What do you need to do to "store up for yourself treasures in heaven" (v. 20)?
❏ make sure I buy a big casket and have them load it with my stuff
❏ invest more time in loving people and less in loving things
❏ give more money to the church and to people in need
❏ talk to more people about Christ
❏ be a better witness to my family
❏ spend more time at church
❏ make Jesus my first priority
❏ other:_____

Option 2 / Epistle Study

1 Timothy 6:3–19 / Planning Ahead

In this passage, Paul summarizes the problem of false teachers and Timothy's role in dealing with them. Read 1 Timothy 6:3–19 and discuss your responses to the following questions with your group.

³If anyone teaches false doctrines and does not agree to the sound instruction of our Lord Jesus Christ and to godly teaching, ⁴he is conceited and understands nothing. He has an unhealthy interest in controversies and quarrels about words that result in envy, strife, malicious talk, evil suspicions ⁵and constant friction between men of corrupt mind, who have been robbed of the truth and who think that godliness is a means to financial gain.

⁶But godliness with contentment is great gain. ⁷For we brought nothing into the world, and we can take nothing out of it. ⁸But if we have food and clothing, we will be content with that. ⁹People who want to get rich fall into temptation and a trap and into many foolish and harmful desires that plunge men into ruin and destruction. ¹⁰For the love of money is a root of all kinds of evil. Some people, eager for money, have wandered from the faith and pierced themselves with many griefs.

¹¹But you, man of God, flee from all this, and pursue righteousness, godliness, faith, love, endurance and gentleness. ¹²Fight the good fight of the faith. Take hold of the eternal life to which you were called when you made your good confession in the presence of many witnesses. ¹³In the sight of God, who gives life to everything, and of Christ Jesus, who while testifying before Pontius Pilate made the good confession, I charge you ¹⁴to keep this command without spot or blame until the appearing of our Lord Jesus Christ, ¹⁵which God will bring about in his own time—God, the blessed and only Ruler, the King of kings and Lord of lords, ¹⁶who alone is immortal and who lives in unapproachable light, whom no one has seen or can see. To him be honor and might forever. Amen.

¹⁷Command those who are rich in this present world not to be arrogant nor to put their hope in wealth, which is so uncertain, but to put their hope in God, who richly provides us with everything for our enjoyment. ¹⁸Command them to do good, to be rich in good deeds, and to be generous and willing to share. ¹⁹In this way they will lay up treasure for themselves as a firm foundation for the coming age, so that they may take hold of the life that is truly life.

1. What was your first job and how much money did you make?

2. What material things do you need at this point in your life in order to be content?

"I've never seen a hearse pulling a U-haul!"
—Charles Swindoll

3. What is the "great gain" in "godliness with contentment" (see notes on v. 6)?

4. What is dangerous about wanting to be rich (see vv. 9–10)?

5. Is there a difference between loving money and enjoying money (see vv. 10 and 17, and notes on v. 17)?

6. What is Paul saying to people who have money, particularly in verses 17–19?

7. If you're really honest, what percentage of your hope is in wealth, and what percentage of your hope is in God?

8. What is your biggest concern about money right now?

9. How do you think the desire for wealth could cause you to "fall into temptation and a trap" (v. 9)?

 # Caring Time / 15–45 Minutes

Take time at the close to share any personal prayer requests. Answer the question:

"How can we help you in prayer this week?"

Then go around and let each person pray for the person on their right. Finish the sentence,

"Dear God, I want to speak to you about my friend _____."

LEADER: Ask the group, "Who are you going to invite next week?"

As you close, include a prayer for the bonding of your group members, as well as for the numerical growth of the group.

Reference Notes

Summary. In the context of this letter, Paul summarizes the problem of false teachers and Timothy's role in dealing with them. In the process, he provides some more details about the false teachers. It turns out that what motivates them is pride, a love of arguments, and greed (vv. 3–5). However, what really ought to motivate us, Paul says, is "godliness with contentment" (vv. 6–10). Every time Paul brings up the problem of the false teachers he then immediately follows up with a word of exhortation to Timothy. Having discussed the false teachers in verses 3–10, even though he has more to say about wealth (vv. 17–19), he injects verses 11–16 in which he makes a final appeal to Timothy.

6:3 *false doctrines.* Paul returns to the theme with which he began his letter (1:3). The false teachers have departed from the teaching of Jesus (see also 1:10; 4:6).

6:5 *godliness is a means to financial gain.* As Paul has hinted in 3:3 and 8, the bottom line motivation of these false teachers is the money they make from their teaching. Paul does not consider it wrong for a person to be paid for teaching (see 5:17–18), but he is incensed when greed is the main motivation for ministry.

6:6–10 Paul picks up on this problem of greed and says two things about it. First, godliness is to be much preferred to profit (vv. 6–8), and second, a love of money brings dire results (vv. 9–10).

6:6 This verse stands in immediate contrast to the last words in verse 5, with a striking play on terms. *They* think godliness "is a way to become rich." Well (in Greek, *de*, meaning "indeed"), they are right. There *is* great profit (now used metaphorically) in godliness (religion does make a person very rich), provided it is accompanied by a "contented spirit" (Moffatt, Kelly); that is, if one is satisfied with what one has and does not seek material gain (Fee).

contentment. This was a favorite word of the Stoic philosophers from whom Paul borrowed it. (Zeno, the founder of this philosophical school, came from Tarsus, Paul's hometown.) This word refers to a person who is not impacted by circumstances. Such a person is self-contained and thus able to rise above all conditions. For Paul, however, this sort of contentment was derived from the Lord (see Phil. 4:11).

6:7–8 There are two reasons why "godliness with contentment" brings great gain. First, at death people can take nothing with them: So why worry about material gain that has to be given up in the end anyway? Second, if people have the essentials in life, this should be enough.

6:9–10 Paul ends by pointing out the dangers of riches. In these verses, he chronicles the downward process that begins with the desire "to get rich." Such a desire leads into "temptation," which is, in turn, "a trap." The "trap" is the "many foolish and harmful desires" that afflict the greedy person. The end result is that such people are "plunge(d) into ruin and destruction."

6:9 *temptation.* Greed causes people to notice and desire what they might not otherwise have paid attention to.

6:10 *For the love of money is a root of all kinds of evil.* Paul is probably quoting a well-known proverb in order to support the assertion he makes in verse 9 that the desire for money leads to ruin. This verse is often misquoted as "money is the root of all evil." While Paul clearly sees the danger of money, he is not contending that *all* evil can be traced to avarice.

Some people … have wandered. Here is the problem. Some of the false teachers have given in to the temptation to riches. They were probably once good leaders in the church but they got caught by Satan (4:1–2), became enamored with speculative ideas (6:3–5), and in the end were pulled down by their love for money.

6:11 *pursue.* Timothy is to *run away from* ("flee") the behavior and attitudes of the false teachers, and instead *go toward* ("pursue") those virtues that reflect the Gospel. Paul names six traits that Timothy is to cultivate.

righteousness. This can be translated "integrity." It refers to upright conduct (see Phil. 1:11).

godliness. This is the same word that is used in 3:16 and 4:7–8; 6:5–6. It refers to a person's relationship to God, especially as it shows itself in outward behavior. This word might also be translated "piety"—though "piety" has a somewhat negative connotation today, which is not the sense of the word as it is used here.

faith, love. These two virtues regularly appear together in the Pastoral Epistles (see 1:5; 2:15; 4:12; 2 Tim. 2:22; Titus 2:2).

endurance. Paul is not urging a passive attitude to life but rather a kind of active, overcoming constancy in the face of trial.

gentleness. This is the kind of spirit in people which means that they do not defend themselves, but yet they are deeply concerned when others are wronged (see also Gal. 5:23; Eph. 4:2; and Col. 3:12).

6:12 *Fight the good fight.* Paul uses an athletic metaphor to encourage Timothy to persevere in the faith. The verb tense emphasizes that this is an ongoing struggle.

Take hold of eternal life. The focus shifts from the contest to the prize. The verb in this case is an aorist imperative, which suggests that a person can grasp eternal life via a single act.

6:17–19 The preceding doxology with its exalted language in praise of God would have provided a fine ending to this letter. But Paul realizes that he must say a few more words about riches, lest he be misunderstood. In verses 9–10, he said some very strong things about money. His concern there was with the false teachers and their use of "godliness [as] a means to financial gain" (v. 5). However, what about those who were already rich? To them Paul says: "Do not place your ultimate trust in your wealth. It is part of this world that is passing away. Place your trust in God and be generous in sharing your wealth."

6:17 *those who are rich.* This is the only place in his letters that Paul addresses the wealthy directly. His consistent "command" is that the rich share their wealth with the poor (see also Rom. 12:8,13; 2 Cor. 9:6–15). "The whole teaching of the Christian ethic is not that wealth is a sin, but that wealth is a very great responsibility" (Barclay).

not to be arrogant nor to put their hope in wealth. These are the twin dangers of wealth—that it will cause people to think themselves to be better than others, and that they might put their trust in their riches (and not in God).

for our enjoyment. But Paul is no ascetic. That the wealthy should not place confidence in their wealth does not carry with it an attitude of total rejection. God, he says, "generously gives us everything for our enjoyment" (see also 4:3–4; Eccl. 5:19–20). *Enjoyment,* however, does not mean self-indulgent living (5:6). The reason *everything* may be enjoyed lies in the recognition that everything, including one's wealth, is a *gift,* the expression of God's gracious generosity (Fee).

6:18 In this verse, Paul tells the rich in four different ways to share their wealth.

SESSION
6

Relationships

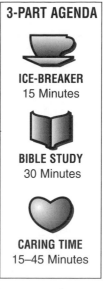

3-PART AGENDA

ICE-BREAKER
15 Minutes

BIBLE STUDY
30 Minutes

CARING TIME
15–45 Minutes

Barbra Streisand sang, "People who need people are the luckiest people in the world." A significant part of our lives is spent in relationship with others. In today's world (where many books, talk show topics, etc. deal with the self and self-fulfillment), we as Christians are called to examine our relationships with others. Again, the perspective of our culture conflicts with God's perspective.

As we set our moral and spiritual compass straight and change from the inside out, we develop a healthy interdependence. One of the goals of incorporating God's core values into our lives is to help us mature. Maturity involves moving from a life of dependence (the emphasis is on "you"), to a life of independence (the emphasis is on "I"), and ultimately to a life of interdependence (the emphasis is on "we").

> **LEADER: This is the next to last session in this course. At the end of the course, how would you like to celebrate your time together? With a dinner? With a party? With a commitment to continue as a group?**

In the Option 1 Study (from Matthew's Gospel), Jesus instructs us on the way we are to be in relationship with others and with God. In the Option 2 Study, James reminds us that we are to treat others as we want to be treated, and that relationships are a higher priority than our own desires.

To get started, take a few minutes to think about your various relationships by doing the following ice-breaker.

Ice-Breaker / 15 Minutes

Relationship Checkup. How are you doing in your relationships? Choose a circle of relationships, such as friends, family, coworkers, etc. From the following choices, select the answer(s) which best describes your recent behavior in the relationships you have chosen. Take turns sharing your answers with the group. Then take turns sharing how you think the other people in that circle of relationships might have seen you.

MISTER ROGERS: I couldn't be nicer.

MICKEY MOUSE: I listen so much, I'm all ears!

DAVID LETTERMAN: I make people laugh.

A DOORMAT: People have been wiping their feet on me.

A TEDDY BEAR: I seem to comfort people.

A GRIZZLY BEAR: Watch out! I might bite!

ALADDIN'S GENIE: All I do is grant other people's wishes.

SCROOGE: Keep your hands off my stuff!

BENEDICT ARNOLD: I feel like a traitor.

DRACULA: People are afraid of me.

Bible Study / 30 Minutes

Option 1 / Gospel Study

Matthew 7:1–12 / Judge or Judged?

In this part of the Sermon on the Mount, Jesus addresses our attitudes toward others and toward God. Read Matthew 7:1–12 and discuss your responses to the following questions with your group.

7 *"Do not judge, or you too will be judged. ²For in the same way you judge others, you will be judged, and with the measure you use, it will be measured to you.*

³"Why do you look at the speck of sawdust in your brother's eye and pay no attention to the plank in your own eye? ⁴How can you say to your brother, 'Let me take the speck out of your eye,' when all the time there is a plank in your own eye? ⁵You hypocrite, first take the plank out of your own eye, and then you will see clearly to remove the speck from your brother's eye.

⁶"Do not give dogs what is sacred; do not throw your pearls to pigs. If you do, they may trample them under their feet, and then turn and tear you to pieces.

⁷"Ask and it will be given to you; seek and you will find; knock and the door will be opened to you. ⁸For everyone who asks receives; he who seeks finds; and to him who knocks, the door will be opened.

⁹"Which of you, if his son asks for bread, will give him a stone? ¹⁰Or if he asks for a fish, will give him a snake? ¹¹If you, then, though you are evil, know how to give good gifts to your children, how much more will your Father in heaven give good gifts to those who ask him! ¹²So in everything, do to others what you would have them do to you, for this sums up the Law and the Prophets."

1. What stands out to you initially in this passage?
- ❐ I'd better clean up my act before I try to clean up someone else's.
- ❐ I'd better keep my mouth shut.
- ❐ I can get anything I want from God—all I need to do is ask.
- ❐ I should treat others the way I want to be treated.

2. Psychologists tell us that we often see in others the very faults we have in ourselves. Do you agree or disagree with this statement?
- ❐ I don't agree—people tend to see the best in others.
- ❐ I agree in part—people tend to judge others fairly, regardless of their faults.
- ❐ I agree—people point out faults in others that they have themselves.
- ❐ I really agree—judgmental people are the people with the most faults.

3. With which of the following persons are you likely to be most—and least—judgmental?
- ❐ my spouse
- ❐ my children
- ❐ other family members
- ❐ my friends
- ❐ people at work
- ❐ people at church
- ❐ elected officials
- ❐ celebrities
- ❐ Christians in general
- ❐ non-Christians in general
- ❐ myself

4. What is "the plank in your own eye" that has sometimes kept you from being able to see others clearly?
- ❐ my excessive sensitivity
- ❐ my desire to be in control
- ❐ my guilt
- ❐ my lack of concern for others
- ❐ my tendency to feel like a martyr
- ❐ my inability to see how I project myself
- ❐ my desire to feel as good as or better than others
- ❐ not really listening
- ❐ my defensiveness
- ❐ my temper
- ❐ my selfishness

5. In verses 7–12, the focus shifts to our relationship with God. What central truth about God does Jesus stress here?

❏ God is merciful and gracious.

❏ God is like Santa Claus—rewarding those who are "good."

❏ God cares for his own.

❏ God cares for everyone.

❏ God gives us a "blank check" through prayer.

❏ God responds to sincere prayer.

6. How would you describe your prayer life lately?

❏ standing on the outside, afraid to knock

❏ casually tapping on the door, but not really expecting an answer

❏ knocking hard, desperate for the door to open

❏ trying to figure out where the door is

❏ not really feeling a need for this door

❏ inside the door, talking to God

7. Which of the following "Golden Rules" do you live by?

❏ "Do to others what you would have them do to you."

❏ "Do it to others, before they do it to you."

❏ "Don't do anything for others, because they won't do anything for you."

❏ "Ignore others and they will ignore you."

❏ "Do to others only what they do to you."

❏ "Wait until someone does something for you, then do something for them."

8. If Jesus were by your side and you could tell him one thing that you wanted to change in your relationships, what would you tell him?

COMMENT

Jesus makes two points about our relationships with each other, and two points about our relationship with God. Concerning our relationships with others: Jesus teaches that while a judgmental, condemning attitude has no place in the life of his followers, discernment is needed. To continually share the Gospel message with those who are adamantly opposed to it is only to invite abuse. Concerning our relationship with God: we are encouraged to pray continuously in confidence that God desires to meet our needs. And the way a good father treats his children is how God treats us.

"When one knows oneself well, one is not desirous of looking into the faults of others."
—John Moschus

50

James 4:1–12 / Life Together

James, like Jesus, had some pretty strong things to say about relationships—both with people and with God. Read James 4:1–12 and share your responses to the following questions with your group.

4 *What causes fights and quarrels among you? Don't they come from your desires that battle within you?* ²*You want something but don't get it. You kill and covet, but you cannot have what you want. You quarrel and fight. You do not have, because you do not ask God.* ³*When you ask, you do not receive, because you ask with wrong motives, that you may spend what you get on your pleasures.*

⁴*You adulterous people, don't you know that friendship with the world is hatred toward God? Anyone who chooses to be a friend of the world becomes an enemy of God.* ⁵*Or do you think Scripture says without reason that the spirit he caused to live in us envies intensely?* ⁶*But he gives us more grace. That is why Scripture says:*

> *"God opposes the proud*
> *but gives grace to the humble."*

⁷*Submit yourselves, then, to God. Resist the devil, and he will flee from you.* ⁸*Come near to God and he will come near to you. Wash your hands, you sinners, and purify your hearts, you double-minded.* ⁹*Grieve, mourn and wail. Change your laughter to mourning and your joy to gloom.* ¹⁰*Humble yourselves before the Lord, and he will lift you up.*

¹¹*Brothers, do not slander one another. Anyone who speaks against his brother or judges him speaks against the law and judges it. When you judge the law, you are not keeping it, but sitting in judgment on it.* ¹²*There is only one Lawgiver and Judge, the one who is able to save and destroy. But you— who are you to judge your neighbor?*

1. Who did you quarrel with the most when you were growing up?

2. Who do you quarrel with the most now? What do you tend to quarrel with that person (or those persons) about?

3. According to verses 1–3, what is at the root of fights and quarrels? What are the reasons we don't have what we want?

4. What is your usual response when your desires are frustrated?
   - ❏ I fight and quarrel.
   - ❏ I throw a fit.
   - ❏ I commit it to God.
   - ❏ I covet what I don't have.
   - ❏ I give up.
   - ❏ I persevere 'til I get what I want.
   - ❏ I say, "I didn't want it anyway."
   - ❏ other:_____

5. We can either be a "friend of the world" (v. 4) or a friend of God. Wha does each friendship mean?

6. How does following verses 7–10 improve our relationship with God?

7. What is the difference between slander or judgmentalism (v. 11) and identifying sin in order to stand against it?

8. Which of the following relational problems are you most likely to be guilty of?
   ❏ fighting and quarreling (vv. 1–2)
   ❏ coveting what someone else has (v. 2)
   ❏ allowing myself to be influenced in a "worldly" way by others (v. 4)
   ❏ slandering, speaking against, or judging others (v. 11)

9. As a response to this study, what step will you take in the coming week to improve your relationships with others and/or your relation ship with God.

> *"The world is a net; the more we stir in it, the more we are entangled."*
> —Proverb

Caring Time / 15–45 Minutes

Take time at the close to share any personal prayer requests Answer the question:

"How can we help you in prayer this week?"

Then go around and let each person pray for the person on their right Finish the sentence:

"Lord, I want to speak to you about my friend _____."

Reference Notes

Summary. This is the third and final part of James' discussion about wis dom. Here he applies his insights to the question of their community lif together as a church. Their failure to live out God's wisdom has had th most serious consequences for them as a church.

4:1–3 James begins by naming the root cause of all this strife. It is th desire for pleasure.

4:1 *fights and quarrels.* Literally, "wars and battles." These are long-term conflicts, not sudden explosions.

desires. Literally, "pleasures." In Greek the word is *hedone*, from which our word "hedonism" is derived. James is not saying that personal pleasure is inherently wrong. However, there is a certain desire for gratification that springs from the wrong source and seems to possess a person in the pursuit for its fulfillment.

within you. The struggle is within a person between the part of him or her which is controlled by the Holy Spirit and that which is controlled by the world.

4:2 *kill and covet.* This is how frustrated desire responds. It lashes out at others in anger and abuse. (This "killing" is in a metaphorical sense—see Matt. 5:21–22.) It responds in jealousy to those who have what it wants.

quarrel and fight. But still they do not have what they desire, so the hostile action continues. The point is that this mad desire-driven quest causes a person to disregard other people, trampling over them if necessary to get what is wanted.

you do not ask God. One reason for this frustrated desire is a lack of prayer.

4:3 James senses a protest: "But I did ask God and I didn't get it." So he qualifies the absolute assertion in verse 2. The desire expressed in prayer may be inappropriate. God will not grant this type of request. Christians pray "in the name of Jesus," implying submission to the will of God. They can ask for wisdom and always expect to get it (if they do not waver), as James explains in 1:5. But this is quite different than asking for something to satisfy an illicit pleasure and always expecting to get it. Prayer is not magic.

spend. This is the same word used in Luke 15:14 to describe the profligate behavior of the prodigal son.

4:4 *friendship with the world.* Rather than living in God's way, in the light of God's wisdom, his people are being molded by the values and desires of secular culture. They have, as it were, crossed over into the enemy's camp and decided to live there.

4:5 This is a most difficult verse to translate, as the footnote in the NIV text indicates. There is a further problem: It is not clear to which verse in Scripture James is referring. Perhaps it is just an allusion to what Scripture says in general about jealousy. In any case, this verse would stand as a warning that what they are doing by forming this allegiance with the world is very dangerous.

4:6 But their case is not hopeless. God does give grace. Repentance is possible. They can turn from their misbehavior.

4:7–10 James now tells them how to repent by means of a series of 10 commands. He has switched to the imperative voice: "Do this," he says "and you will escape the mess you have gotten yourselves in." He tells them to submit, resist, come near, wash, purify, grieve, mourn, wail, change, and humble themselves.

4:7 *Submit yourselves, then, to God.* His first and primary command is that they must submit to God. It is not too surprising that James says this since what these Christians have been doing is resisting God and his ways. As James just pointed out, it is the humble who receive God's grace. A proud person is unwilling to submit and therefore not open to grace, feeling that he or she needs nothing.

Resist the devil. Submission to God begins with resistance to Satan. Thus far they have been giving in to the devil's enticements. A clear sign of their new lifestyle will be this inner resistance to devilish desires.

he will flee from you. Since Satan has no ultimate power over a Christian, when resisted he can do little but withdraw.

4:9 True repentance will often show itself in strong feelings of grief. James is not urging asceticism as a lifestyle. Rather, he is teaching about the dynamics of repentance (see Jer. 4:8 and Joel 2:12–14).

Grieve. This word originally described "the experience of an army whose food has gone and who have no shelter for the stormy weather" (Barclay).

mourn and wail. When people realize that they have been leading self centered lives, in disobedience to God and harmful to others, they often feel overwhelming grief at what they have done.

4:10 *Humble.* This last command urges humility before God as did the first command ("Submit to God").

4:11–12 James ends his section on wisdom and speech by moving from a general call to repentance (vv. 7–10) to a specific form of wrongdoing that they must deal with. His focus is on the sin of judgment and the pride that underlies it.

P.S.
If the next session is your last session together, you may want to plan party to celebrate your time together. Save a few minutes at the close of this session to make these plans.

SESSION

7

Choices

3-PART AGENDA

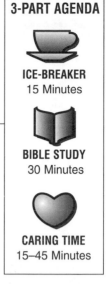

ICE-BREAKER
15 Minutes

BIBLE STUDY
30 Minutes

CARING TIME
15–45 Minutes

We live in a world that is full of choices. In his book *Future Shock*, Alvin Toffler coined the word "over-choice" to describe people who feel they have too many choices (in fact, so many that they are hard to make). But making the little choices becomes easier once we have made the big choices: What road are we going to take, and who are we going to follow? We have many values to choose from in life. But once we choose to follow Christ and his way, those value decisions begin to fall in place. The values we choose are part of our commitment to Christ, and they serve as an anchor in the midst of the hard times which come to each person's life. When everything around us seems about to fall, we can hold firm to Christ and the eternal values we have through him.

> **LEADER: Read the bottom part of page M8 in the center section concerning future mission possibilities for your group. Save plenty of time for the evaluation and future planning during the Caring Time. You will need to be prepared to lead this important discussion.**

What we have at the end will be far greater than the sum of all of the parts. To the world, the culmination is achieving everything we want in life—reaching the top. But for the Christian (who looks at life through a different paradigm), the culmination is two-fold: weathering the storms of life in this world, and anticipating the world which is to come. For us, fulfillment occurs when we choose the way of the Gospel, change from the inside out, and incorporate the radically challenging values of Christ into our daily life.

In the following studies, we will see that Christians are called to a special lifestyle. In the Option 1 Study (from Matthew's Gospel), Jesus instructs us to choose the narrow gate and path—understanding that these will lead to true life. Using another analogy, he tells us what we are choosing in him is a solid foundation on which to build, one that can weather any storm. In the Option 2 Study (from 1 Corinthians), Paul calls us to continue to build on that solid foundation in our own unique way.

Ice-Breaker / 15 Minutes

Valued Values. Begin this last session of your study together with an affirmation exercise. Below is a list of qualities based on the positive values in this course. In silence, think about the members of your group and jot down their names next to the value that describes them best. Ask one person to sit in silence while the others explain which value they selected for that individual. Then go to the next person and do the same until everyone is affirmed.

_____PURE IN HEART: Your life is marked with integrity before God and other people.

_____PEACEMAKER: You have a gift from God to help people overcome their differences.

_____TRANSPARENT: You can be yourself without any pretenses and let the light of Christ shine through you.

_____FAITHFUL: You are faithful to uphold God's morality even under pressure.

_____MERCIFUL / COMPASSIONATE: You have the ability to feel what others feel; to be happy or to hurt with them.

_____SPIRITUALLY HUNGRY: I admire the longing in your heart for a growing, genuine relationship with God.

_____ALWAYS LOVING: You have a Christlike capacity to love others unconditionally—no matter what.

_____COMMUNITY BUILDER: God uses you as a bond to bring people together in unity.

_____HUMBLE: I admire the quiet way you demonstrate what humility is all about.

_____GENEROUS: You give freely, not for attention or praise—but for the simple joy of giving.

_____CONTENTED: You know your worth is based on who you are rather than what you have.

_____JOYFUL: Regardless of the circumstances, you have a smile on your face and a positive outlook about life

_____PATIENT: You never seem to be in a hurry or to get irritated by others.

Bible Study / 30 Minutes

Option 1 / Gospel Study

Matthew 7:13–27 / Building Plans

The Sermon on the Mount is concluded by four contrasts in which Jesus urges people to choose between commitment to him and the way of the world. There are only two ways, two kinds of teachers, two kinds of followers and two kinds of foundations. Read Matthew 7:13–27 and discuss your responses to the following questions with your group.

[13]"Enter through the narrow gate. For wide is the gate and broad is the road that leads to destruction, and many enter through it. [14]But small is the gate and narrow the road that leads to life, and only a few find it.

[15]"Watch out for false prophets. They come to you in sheep's clothing, but inwardly they are ferocious wolves. [16]By their fruit you will recognize them. Do people pick grapes from thornbushes, or figs from thistles? [17]Likewise every good tree bears good fruit, but a bad tree bears bad fruit. [18]A good tree cannot bear bad fruit, and a bad tree cannot bear good fruit. [19]Every tree that does not bear good fruit is cut down and thrown into the fire. [20]Thus, by their fruit you will recognize them.

[21]"Not everyone who says to me, 'Lord, Lord,' will enter the kingdom of heaven, but only he who does the will of my Father who is in heaven. [22]Many will say to me on that day, 'Lord, Lord, did we not prophesy in your name, and in your name drive out demons and perform many miracles?' [23]Then I will tell them plainly, 'I never knew you. Away from me, you evildoers!'

[24]"Therefore everyone who hears these words of mine and puts them into practice is like a wise man who built his house on the rock. [25]The rain came down, the streams rose, and the winds blew and beat against that house; yet it did not fall, because it had its foundation on the rock. [26]But everyone who hears these words of mine and does not put them into practice is like a foolish man who built his house on sand. [27]The rain came down, the streams rose, and the winds blew and beat against that house, and it fell with a great crash."

1. Which short phrase captures the mood of this passage best?
  ❏ Watch out! ❏ Just do it!
  ❏ Be prepared! ❏ Walk your talk!

2. What does "the rock" represent in verse 24?
  ❏ the truth of the Gospel ❏ obedience to Jesus' words
  ❏ faith in Jesus ❏ other:_____
  ❏ Jesus himself

"God's way becomes plain when we start walking in it."
—Roy L. Smith

3. Mark an *"X"* on the lines below to describe the "ways" you have chosen to live your life?

broad road:
going with the flow _____ narrow road:
going against the flow

focus on
outward appearances _____ focus on
inward changes

longing for
material things _____ longing
for God

focus on
personal pleasures _____ focus on
commitment to others

critical
of others _____ finding the best
in others

inner chaos _____ inner peace

4. Who are the "false prophets" that you need to be on your guard against?
   ❏ the religious establishment
   ❏ cults, New Age movement, other religions
   ❏ those who have "fallen" in the Christian world
   ❏ friends who don't have Christian values
   ❏ other:_____

5. What is Jesus promising those who are willing to live by his words?
   ❏ You will never experience storms.
   ❏ You will experience the same storms as everyone else.
   ❏ The storms will not destroy your faith.
   ❏ You will get a new house if your old one collapses.

6. One thing that has helped me withstand storms has been:
   ❏ a strong family   ❏ a strong self-reliance
   ❏ God's spiritual family   ❏ a strong faith in God
   ❏ great friends   ❏ a sense of humor
   ❏ knowing tomorrow is another day ❏ other:_____

7. The sand which I have sometimes built my life on has been:
   ❏ my own abilities, resources or goodness
   ❏ pleasing others
   ❏ materialism—basing my happiness on things
   ❏ pleasure—basing my happiness on good times
   ❏ trendy philosophies
   ❏ apathy—just going with the crowd
   ❏ other:_____

8. How would you describe your spiritual foundation right now?

☐ shaky   ☐ slipping

☐ solid   ☐ rebuilding

☐ brand new   ☐ other:_____

9. In order to build on "rock" for my future, what I need to do most is:

☐ learn more about growing in my faith

☐ practice what I've already learned

☐ change my priorities in life

☐ stop worrying so much about what others think

☐ plan for my future instead of acting on impulse

☐ focus on my inner life rather than the externals of life

☐ listen for God's voice and leading in my life

☐ other:_____

Option 2 / Epistle Study

1 Corinthians 3:1–23 / A Piece of the Rock

Paul instructs the church of Corinth on the way to build their lives and their church on a solid foundation. Read 1 Corinthians 3:1–23 and discuss your responses to the following questions with your group.

3 Brothers, I could not address you as spiritual but as worldly—mere infants in Christ. ²I gave you milk, not solid food, for you were not yet ready for it. Indeed, you are still not ready. ³You are still worldly. For since there is jealousy and quarreling among you, are you not worldly? Are you not acting like mere men? ⁴For when one says, "I follow Paul," and another, "I follow Apollos," are you not mere men?

⁵What, after all, is Apollos? And what is Paul? Only servants, through whom you came to believe—as the Lord has assigned to each his task. ⁶I planted the seed, Apollos watered it, but God made it grow. ⁷So neither he who plants nor he who waters is anything, but only God, who makes things grow. ⁸The man who plants and the man who waters have one purpose, and each will be rewarded according to his own labor. ⁹For we are God's fellow workers; you are God's field, God's building.

¹⁰By the grace God has given me, I laid a foundation as an expert builder, and someone else is building on it. But each one should be careful how he builds. ¹¹For no one can lay any foundation other than the one already laid, which is Jesus Christ. ¹²If any man builds on this foundation using gold, silver, costly stones, wood, hay or straw, ¹³his work will be shown for what it is, because the Day will bring it to light. It will be revealed with fire, and the fire will test the quality of each man's work. ¹⁴If what he has built survives, he will receive his reward. ¹⁵If it is burned up, he will suffer loss; he himself will be saved, but only as one escaping through the flames.

16Don't you know that you yourselves are God's temple and that God's Spirit lives in you? 17If anyone destroys God's temple, God will destroy him; for God's temple is sacred, and you are that temple.

18Do not deceive yourselves. If any one of you thinks he is wise by the standards of this age, he should become a "fool" so that he may become wise. 19For the wisdom of this world is foolishness in God's sight. As it is written: "He catches the wise in their craftiness"; 20and again, "The Lord knows that the thoughts of the wise are futile." 21So then, no more boasting about men! All things are yours, 22whether Paul or Apollos or Cephas or the world or life or death or the present or the future—all are yours, 23and you are of Christ, and Christ is of God.

1. When you were a child, what did you grow or make that you were proud of?

2. Who are the key people God has used to lead you to become a believer? Who was the "Paul" who first planted the seed of God's Word in your life? Who was the "Apollos" who watered the seed and helped it grow?

3. According to Paul, what is the one and only foundation in life (v. 11)? Does that seem a little narrow-minded to you?

"If we build to please ourselves, we are building on the sand; if we build for the love of God, we are building on the rock."
—Oswald Chambers

4. What do the building materials in verse 12 refer to (see notes on v. 12)?

5. How confident are you that your "building materials" will pass the fire test of verse 13?

6. How does it make you feel to hear that, as God's church, "you yourselves are God's temple and that God's Spirit lives in you" (v. 16)? How can remembering this help you make better choices in life?

7. What is God's view of the "wisdom of this world" (vv. 19–20)?

8. In the last year, would you say your spiritual "building" has gotten weaker or stronger?

9. What can you do to assure that what you build from now on will be quality work (able to stand the test)?
   ❏ focus less on material things and more on spiritual things
   ❏ focus less on the world's wisdom and more on God's wisdom
   ❏ pray for guidance and strength to live a holy life
   ❏ stay in a group like this that will hold me accountable
   ❏ spend more time in valuable activities like "planting seeds" to help others grow in their faith
   ❏ other:_____

Caring Time / 15–45 Minutes

EVALUATION

1. Take some time to evaluate the life of your group by using the statements below. Read the first sentence out loud and ask everyone to explain where they would put a dot between the two extremes. When you are finished, go back and give your group an overall grade in the categories of Group Building, Bible Study and Mission.

 **GROUP BUILDING**

On celebrating life and having fun together, we were more like a ...
wet blanket _____hot tub

On becoming a caring community, we were more like a ...
prickly porcupine _____cuddly teddy bear

 **BIBLE STUDY**

On sharing our spiritual stories, we were more like a ...
shallow pond _____spring-fed lake

On digging into Scripture, we were more like a ...
slow-moving snail _____voracious anteater

○→○ **MISSION**

On inviting new people into our group, we were more like a ...
barbed-wire fence _____wide-open door

On stretching our vision for mission, we were more like an ...
ostrich _____eagle

2. What are some specific areas in which you have grown in this course about core values?
☐ growing in my appreciation of God's Word as the standard for my values
☐ increasing my commitment to Jesus Christ and his teachings
☐ desiring to please God in regard to morality, values and choices
☐ being more faithful to God's ideals for my relationships with others
☐ longing to have a more intimate relationship with God
☐ having a vision for how I can be more content in life
☐ other:_____

A covenant is a promise made to each other in the presence of God. Its purpose is to indicate your intention to make yourselves available to one another for the fulfillment of the purposes you share in common. If your group is going to continue, in a spirit of prayer work your way through the following sentences, trying to reach an agreement on each statement pertaining to your ongoing life together. Write out your covenant like a contract, stating your purpose, goals and the ground rules for your group.

1. The purpose of our group will be:

2. Our goals will be:

3. We will meet for _____weeks, after which we will decide if we wish to continue as a group.

4. We will meet from _____ to _____ and we will strive to start on time and end on time.

5. We will meet at _____ (place) or we will rotate from house to house.

6. We will agree to the following ground rules for our group (check):

❒ PRIORITY: While you are in the course, you give the group meetings priority.

❒ PARTICIPATION: Everyone participates and no one dominates.

❒ RESPECT: Everyone is given the right to their own opinion, and all questions are encouraged and respected.

❒ CONFIDENTIALITY: Anything that is said in the meeting is never repeated outside the meeting.

❒ EMPTY CHAIR: The group stays open to new people at every meeting, as long as they understand the ground rules.

❒ SUPPORT: Permission is given to call upon each other in time of need at any time.

❒ ACCOUNTABILITY: We agree to let the members of the group hold us accountable to the commitments which each of us make in whatever loving ways we decide upon.

❒ MISSION: We will do everything in our power to start a new group.

Reference Notes

Summary. Paul returns to the question of factions in the Corinthian church. The problem is that by misunderstanding the nature of wisdom (by viewing the Gospel as if it were just another philosophical system) and then exalting certain teachers, they betray their immaturity as Christians. Instead, the Corinthian Christians need to understand that they are "God's field" and "God's building"; and that Paul, Apollos and the others are mere servants who assist God in bringing about their growth. By pretending to be "wise" (by the standards of the world), they show themselves to be "foolish" (in the eyes of God).

3:1 *Brothers.* Despite his criticism they are still part of the same family. The issue is whether they are mature or immature in their faith.

spiritual. A mature Christian whose life is dominated by the indwelling Spirit.

worldly. Those Christians who are molded more by the spirit of the age than by the Spirit of God; those whose life and thoughts are so immature that they are "mere infants."

3:2 *I gave you milk.* Paul continues his metaphor. When he was in Corinth, they were not yet ready for "solid food."

3:3 Jealousy and quarreling are clear indications that they are still "infants."

mere men. By exalting certain teachers, they betray their lack of understanding of the Gospel. Paul's point is that although they have the Spirit, they are acting precisely like people without the Spirit.

3:5 *servants.* Paul and Apollos are not to be exalted. They are merely servants—this same word is used to describe a waiter. They were just carrying out the task God had given them.

3:6 *I planted.* Paul was the first to preach in Corinth.

Apollos watered. Apollos continued Paul's work by helping to build up a new church.

God made it grow. Their labors alone would not have been enough. The divine life-force necessary to produce growth came from God.

3:9 *God's field.* The Corinthians are the field which God is plowing.

God's building. Paul's metaphor shifts from agriculture to architecture.

3:10 *I laid a foundation.* By preaching Jesus Christ, who is the foundation (v. 11), Paul was the one who began the work in Corinth (v. 6).

expert. Literally, "wise." Paul continues to develop the idea of wisdom.

builder (In Greek, *archiekton*). The one who plans and supervises the construction of a building.

3:11 A community might be built on another foundation, but it would not be the church. The church's only foundation is Jesus Christ (see 1 Cor. 1:18–25).

3:12 Paul describes some of the ways a person can go astray in building on the foundation—namely by using inferior or inadequate materials.

gold, silver, costly stones. These materials will survive the test of fire.

wood, hay or straw. These will burn up.

3:13 ***the Day.*** On the Day of Judgment the quality of labor will be revealed.

revealed with fire. The idea is fire as a means of testing—a way of revealing the "quality of each man's work."

3:16 ***temple.*** Paul tells them what kind of building they as a community are becoming (the reference is not to individual believer's bodies as the temple of the Spirit; that comes in 1 Cor. 6:19). This would be a particularly vivid and exciting image for the Corinthians, surrounded as they were by pagan temples.

3:17 ***destroy.*** The idea has shifted from losing one's pay for having used inferior building materials (vv. 12–15) to being punished for destroying the church. If the Corinthians continue to quarrel, they defile God's holy temple and will be marked for destruction.

3:19 The simple fact is that God's wisdom and the wisdom of the world are at opposite poles. From God's perspective, what the world calls "wisdom" is really "foolishness."

3:21 ***no more boasting about men!*** In the light of this, Paul calls upon them to bring to an end their divisions.

All things are yours. Paul wants the Corinthians to remember that leaders and people are all servants of Christ, destined to be sovereign over all creation. It is not that Christians control the world, life, death, the present and the future (v. 22) in a manipulative sense. The point is that these things no longer have final power over them (Rom. 8:38–39). Ultimately, since they are Christ's and Christ is of God (v. 23), the church will triumph over what once dominated it. In the face of such an amazing truth, it is absurd to continue their petty divisions!